MW01485068

Nourish the Soul

Filling The Emptiness Within

A Memoir

Bracha Goetz

The Goetz Bookshop
& Publishing House
USA

Nourish the Soul © 2023. All rights reserved by The Goetz Bookshop, LLC.

Originally published as
Searching for God in the Garbage © 2017. All rights reserved by Bracha Goetz.

No part of this book may be reproduced or transmitted in any form or by any means, graphic, electronic, or mechanical, including photocopying, recording, taping, or by any informational storage retrieval system without prior permission in writing from the publisher.

The Goetz Bookshop & Publishing House

For information:
The Goetz
Bookshop &
Publishing House
info@goetzbookshop.com
tel.832-377-5656

www.goetzbookshop.com

ISBN: 978-1-7370940-5-0

Book Cover Design: Rachel Bergida

The information in this book is not intended or implied to be a substitute for professional medical advice, diagnosis, or treatment. If you have any type of food addiction resulting in a medical condition you should seek professional advice.

Printed in the United States of America

Let's begin at the end. I became an Orthodox Jew.

This book tells the story of how that happened through actual records I kept, though some details have been changed.

Psalm 113, Verses 7-9

From the trash heaps He lifts up the needy

to seat them with nobles,

with the nobles of His people.

He returns the barren woman to the home,

a joyful mother of children.

Halleluyah!

Chapter One: 1966-1968

June 8, 1966   Class 4-A

Joanne Singer   Mrs. Avidon

"When I Was a Butterfly"

When I was small, not pretty at all,

I wished I could be pretty, pretty and tall.

I made a cocoon, then went inside.

It was so short, not at all wide.

All winter long I cried and I cried.

For I wanted to go back outside.

Finally, here was spring.

I felt myself turning into a wing.

I could not fit in the cocoon anymore,

So I bit and I bit, and I tore and I tore.

Do you know what? I was outside again.

I felt like an egg that popped out of a hen.

I looked all around me. What were these things?

"Oh gosh," I said, "These are my wings!"

I was pink, green, and blue,

A beautiful butterfly, bright and new.

December 22, 1967

Dear Diary,

I am going to call you Twilly for the time being because it sounds magical. It's short for twilight—a time of changes. And I am changing a lot now. I am Joanne Singer and I'm going to be twelve on January 19th. I love to print and not write in script. And I love magical people like Mary Poppins. My favorite food is *kishke*—stuffed derma.

I always thought writing in a diary was dumb, over-girlish, but since then I've changed my mind. One reason is because I'm growing up and the other reason is because I just finished reading *The Diary of Anne Frank*. When I grow up I want to join the Peace Corps and help people in Togo, Africa. Why did I pick that tiny country? I don't know, it just seems like the perfect spot!

I love to think about how long is forever and how long is never. Is there an end to everything, like time? I used to, but now I don't really care what happens after you are dead. Is life just a test?

February 10, 1968

Dear Twilly,

Today was very strange. I am not at all the way I am

writing in this diary. I am what people call "a very popular child." I run around always talking, laughing, teasing, giggling. Everyone likes me. Today I brought out the inner me and switched my outside personality. Nobody liked me. They thought I was odd. Nothing can comfort me or make me forget what's inside.

I will always only be inside my own head. I'll never see the world through someone else's eyes. I wish I could see how Susie and Roberta and Eva and Lisa see. Why can't I be really happy like other people?

Anne Frank wrote: "Riches can all be lost, but that happiness in your own heart can only be veiled, and it will still bring you happiness as long as you live. As long as you can look fearlessly up into the heavens, as long as you know that you are pure within and that you will still find happiness."

I feel pure when I talk to God in my bed, just before I fall asleep. But I am starting not to believe in God anymore.

Was there ever complete peace, love, and belief in God on Earth? If this diary is ever found by someone a long time in the future, please write in this blank space below.

                                        March 4, 1968

Dear Twilly,

A bunch of boys followed me home from school today shouting dirty things over and over. I heard one of them say, "Let's find out if she really does or not." I ran so fast to my apartment building and raced up the three flights of stairs. 'Til I got that key into the door! I was shaking so much.

It feels like overnight I got a different body. How could this happen so suddenly? I'm afraid to go to school tomorrow.

March 8, 1968

Dear Twilly,

I often see someone in a dream drifting farther and farther away, saying, "Don't forget. Don't forget. *Remember.*" But believe it or not, I forgot what it is I'm supposed to remember! It feels like I'm looking for something. I like to wander through the streets. But after a while, I don't know what to do with myself.

What I want most of all is to find who I really am.

April 21, 1968

Dear Twilly,

I hate when my relatives come over because they never ask me about anything important. So I end up slamming my bedroom door and just looking out the window. I talk to My Tree and feel the fresh air, letting my hair fly around my face. I pretend it is country air and sometimes it really smells that way. I put my favorite album on the record player and play only this one song about a woman growing older. It says how young girls' lives are like April, full of changes. "But one day they grow up and April is over forever." I don't know why I love that part of the song. I guess because I feel like April now.

I love my room. I like being alone, but I get lonesome when I am. I have so many problems.

May 4, 1968

Dear Twilly,

My Aunt Trudy has a kosher kitchen in her house. So when we go to Aunt Trudy's and we're in the mood for Chinese food, we get those white containers from Sun Luck's take-out place. We take down the set of *traife* (non-kosher) dishes and silverware that they keep way up on the highest shelves in their kitchen cabinets for these special occasions. Then we set up the bridge table in Aunt Trudy's bedroom and we eat the Chinese food in there.

But before we can start to eat the Chinese food, Aunt Trudy always tells me to make sure the venetian blinds are closed shut on their bedroom windows. It usually feels so secret and sneaky. But today I felt angry when they asked me to do it. What do they think? That God can't see through venetian blinds? I hated all the hypocrisy! But I still ate up all the pork chop suey.

May 30, 1968

Dear Twilly,

I'm not going to stop writing to you. I feel like I'm talking to you although my lips aren't moving. I could never give up these spilling moments. But Twilly, I've been forgetting My Tree lately. This tree has shared my loneliness. And I'm afraid she's very sick now and I don't know what to do for her. What do they do to sick trees on city streets that don't give leaves anymore in the spring? Every morning when I get up I rush to the window to see if any leaves have come, but every branch is empty.

I think she is dying. Will they chop her down? I won't let them. But I'll probably be in school when they do it.

June 2, 1968

Dear Twilly,

I don't like tranquility. It's too quiet. I want more exciting things. I'm very insecure now. I always need something to chew on. I'm afraid to be alone with myself. I have to turn on TV or something. That's why I talk on the telephone so much. I need something secure to grasp. I'm afraid of getting lost in the world. I'm afraid to let myself go.

Writing here makes me understand myself more. But I'm even writing now so I won't find myself alone. I'll be kept busy so I won't think too much.

June 6, 1968

Dear Twilly,

Robert F. Kennedy was shot. Pick someone you don't agree with and kill him. After all, this land has freedom. How could someone kill another human being? I just feel kind of sick of life, with no purpose. All my ideals seem so far off in an evil world like ours. And look at Martin Luther King, Jr. Why should anyone want to try to help this world be better? Look what happens.

Last night I felt left out. Odd, because I was staying out of trouble. All my friends were hanging out in the schoolyard and I wanted to go down and join them. But my parents wouldn't let me. Even though I wouldn't do the junk they were doing. I don't really want to get corrupted. I guess my only dream in life is to find myself.

But then as I looked at all the kids in the schoolyard and how they are all getting corrupted, I thought maybe I *could* understand how easy it can become for people to just pick up a gun and kill someone else.

June 19, 1968

Dear Twilly,

I am shocked at my best friend, Carol. Ugh. How could they all kiss like that? *Why?* How could I have thought of her as my best friend? All that making-out doesn't mean anything. I don't understand why people act like that. Why do people make beautifully created things into dirty, disgusting ones?

I'm afraid to grow up. I don't want to see what it will be like when our generation becomes grown-ups. I want to close my eyes and keep dreaming. My friends take all the joy out of being a kid.

July 3, 1968

Dear Twilly,

Boys aren't that important. I must convince myself. They *aren't*. But they are.

July 15, 1968

Dear Twilly,

We just had another "social" on the boy's side of the camp. Nobody asked me to dance again. I hate going to these things, but they make us. I just sit there the whole time either wishing for someone to ask me to dance or wishing I was invisible. What's wrong with me? Am I really so weird? Maybe they just see how anxious I am to get asked. Even if I try so hard not to look that way. Do they all see that I'm practically sitting on the edge of my chair all the time ready to leap into the arms of any boy who will even look in my direction? I don't see how I can pretend that I'm not interested. What is it that I'm supposed to be doing? Is something very wrong with me?

July 28, 1968

Dear Twilly,

Another social. Not one dance. Will I ever get married?

August 8, 1968

Dear Twilly,

Hi! I was very happy today with a regular kind of life. I had a lot of fun today. Winning the raffle, rolling down the big hill, playing games in the Social Hall, the Peanut Hunt. Is *this* what life is all about? We're supposed to have fun and not think too much?

Love,

Raffle #46!

August 9, 1968

Dear Twilly,

I think regular life is becoming more a part of me. I'm conforming. But I still love quiet, beautiful things. I feel so much closer to people when I find their inner true selves. I love the inner people.

I don't want to put on a false cover smile. I want to know which smiles are real.

But I can also enjoy the "regular life." I love playing this double game. This was The Gigantic Secret being hidden from me! Everyone wears masks.

I see the choice now. Give up my friends and think seriously, living within me, or give up me to have friends. Will I leave myself behind when I grow up? Remember who the real me was?

November 6, 1968

Dear Twilly,

I hate Junior High School. I am so lonely, lost, and confused there. I want to hold onto my past, to elementary school. I'm not happy. I can't look fearlessly up into the heavens and face God. I don't believe in God. And I don't like flirting like the other girls.

December 3, 1968

Dear Twilly,

I'm becoming very different lately. I'm not so nice. I don't want to, but I end up telling strings and strings of lies to my mother. I want to do all the things considered "wrong" by society. I want to be fresh and tough. And trampy.

December 5, 1968

Dear Twilly,

Junior High is very cold. Do some people live in coldness all their lives?

December 9, 1968

Dear Twilly,

My class is a bunch of phonies. But I don't hate them. I'm one too. I wish I didn't have to be.

There's nothing to hold onto. I just have to keep drifting with the waves, drifting far away. There is nothing I believe in or that I can depend on or trust.

Why is it important to go to school? It doesn't teach me anything anymore. Maybe it does…sadness.

Somebody carved some filthy words about me into my desk in homeroom. How come I feel like it's carved into me?

December 20, 1968

Dear Twilly,

We are going to land on the Moon. But that will destroy it. We will stop it from being unreachable in a child's dreamy eyes.

December 31, 1968

Dear Twilly,

The people I see when I stick my head way out my window

at night are my Nighttime People. They are the exciting nighttime life I can't have. They are everyone else in the wide, wide world.

Chapter Two: 1969-1970

January 15, 1969

Dear Twilly,

Junior High is ruining me. But then again, it's stopping me from thinking so much.

Every day feels like when the swimming counselor pushed me off the dock into the water that was above my head. I wasn't ready. She came from behind when I wasn't expecting it. I felt such terror underwater because I had no idea how to rise up out of it.

January 17, 1969

Dear Twilly,

I have lost myself under the phoniness. I'm trying to recover my feelings, but I can't. What's so great anyway, about finding who I am? Someday I'll die anyway. So what if I die as a person I don't know! I haven't had any time to think. I've been rushing around doing nothing lately. Real me, are you still in there?

January 19, 1969

"Behind the Nothingness Lies Something"

So beautiful inside,

so locked up,

unable to pass through the door

so many others

constantly

pass through.

Unable to show

her real feelings

hidden in shadows and

felt like an unforgettable pain…

inside.

Like a clock constantly ticking that

nobody hears.

When it stops ticking

nobody misses it.

February 9, 1969

Dear Twilly,

Today I was the most popular thing on earth. I sort of felt so high that I was falling over. How have I changed? I see the ugliness in life. I've gotten used to it. And I'm becoming ugly, too.

March 3, 1969

"Once upon A Time"

A child on a summer morning can laugh at the silliest thing.

And for no reason at all, she can skip or dance or sing.

A child catching a snowflake can smile when she is glad.

A child watching the leaves fall can cry when she is sad.

A child hearing carousel's music can love without feeling
pain.

A child smelling a flower can make sunshine out of rain.

A child on a summer morning can have all her dreams
come true.

It's so unbelievable to think

that once

this

child

was

you.

March 14, 1969

Dear Twilly,

What if we all were covered with white sheets? Then we
could just touch each other's inner people and not have to

look and judge everybody from the outside.

Please don't let me stop searching. I will find whatever it is someday.

March 15, 1969

"Reach Out In the Darkness and You May Find a Friend"

I reach out and I want a Hand to grab me,

To hold me tight and secure.

I reach out and I want a soul to touch me,

And understand that I'm not being pure.

I reach out and I'm searching for something to grasp,

So that I won't keep sinking.

I reach out and pray for someone to listen,

To share all these thoughts I am thinking.

I reach out and finally find someone

That wants so much to hear,

So I cry on my shoulder,

And comfort each lonely fear.

March 16, 1969

Dear Twilly,

Today I wandered into a Jewish Center that was unlocked and deserted. Most of the time I don't feel God. I don't even believe in God. But I guess part of me keeps hoping.

In the dark synagogue, there was just one bright "eternal light" lit up at the front. The absorbing darkness was scary. I felt as if God's Presence was around me. I felt so small, so nothing and yet part of everything gigantic; a never-beginning and never-ending Universe. I got very frightened in there and I ran out.

What I felt today doesn't seem important enough to tell to anybody. Even though it may be *all* that is important.

March 17, 1969

Dear Twilly,

I think this generation is making people phonier and further apart. And we are rebelling because we think we are doing the opposite. When we grow up, I bet this generation will be even more phony and commercial.

We are all lonely, tired, and searching. We really don't know how to go about changing the world because we want to jump into things without knowing what we are doing. Things like life.

March 22, 1969

Dear Twilly,

I think I'm really very grown up. This is a year for "experimenting." I want to act free. Yesterday I tried smoking. God, do I hope no one reads this. Bye!

March 23, 1969

Dear Twilly,

Last night the principal called my parents because I got in some trouble at school. I wish someone would smother me in warmth. When I stare at myself in the mirror, I don't look the way I feel. I don't look like me at all. Why am I so mixed up?

May 3, 1969

And then I realized that The Choice had come down to me.

It was the moment for me to decide whether I wanted to

become just a member of the crowd,

indistinguishable within a mob,

leading a forgotten life,

like all the others -

Or stand out.

And be someone special and

different,

and make something remembered of my life.

But all I felt around me was this great, secure feeling

of Belonging.

(to at least something, even if it was nothing)

(to at least some people, even if it was not myself)

To something with no feelings, not sad or happy.

Just at least, if nothing else

I would be part of

Humanity.

A feeling that you are not alone,

Even if you are.

And then I realized, too late, that The Choice had been decided. I screamed with all my soul and let out everything. The people passed me on the street and shook their heads at the "crazy girl" on the corner. And when I saw this, I sort of laughed between my tears, catching the sad joke. It was a "different" kind of way to say good-bye to being different.

June 2, 1969

Dear Twilly,

School means so little to me now. I love getting on the subway and going to Central Park. Hanging out there is so exciting and free. I have learned that if you're very quiet and obedient and follow all the rules, you won't have any fun. You've got to enjoy yourself and really live! You also have to let yourself go and not feel inhibited.

I cut school again today! Bye!

June 5, 1969

Dear Twilly,

Hi! Everything is *so great*! I'm having so much fun. I have so many friends that really like me. All I want to do is suck up as many friends as I can get. I think I have the most friends in the seventh grade. To be popular, like in politics, you have to be very clever and phony. My phone never stops ringing.

I gave a report on "Peace" today at school. It was great! I'm cutting school and going to a Peace Rally on Wednesday. Everything is so cool! But still something is missing. I'm missing something like crazy.

June 19, 1969

Dear Twilly,

I grew up a lot last night. I saw some other worlds exist that I don't yet know much about. I think the worlds end wherever you want.

Have fun, Twil!

September 2, 1969

Hi Twil!

I'm back! I went camping out this summer all across the country with a teen tour. We had a van and a tent and we had a blast. All the way out to California. I was the youngest in our group and everyone called me the "flower child." We were all into being free and natural and loving everybody.

We slept in youth hostels and also in parks and on beaches. I loved the Haight-Ashbury scene. One day, out in San Francisco, though, we ate lunch in the fanciest hotel, The Fairmont, and we took some of their fancy silverware back with us afterwards, as "souvenirs"! Oh, it was so much fun!

One rainy night we camped out in this laundromat and one night we slept in a church. And I slept in the first row of the church in one of those velvet pews. So when I opened my eyes in the morning, I saw J.C. standing over me, standing *right* over me, all stretched out on the cross. The first thought I had was that I had died. And then the second thought I had was, *"Oh no! I am in the wrong religion!"* It was really far out!

January 13, 1970

Dear Twilly,

I hate my parents so much. How could they do this to me? They showed up at the party last night. They drove over there, and in the middle of the party, walked right into the apartment, waiting until I left with them. How could they do such a thing? Nobody else's parents care. Why do I have to have embarrassing parents like this? I feel like such a goody-goody jerk. How can I face my friends now?

January 16, 1970

Dear Twilly,

I feel beautiful and ugly at the same time. Everyone makes me feel so beautiful. I make myself feel ugly. I know when I'll look back on these pages, I'll think it was funny that I was writing all these things when I was really so young. But *please* try to remember I was. I *am* more alive now, at almost fourteen, than I'll probably ever be again. I am still secretly alive.

February 1970/ 50 cents

McCall's Magazine

"A Space for Silences"

My grandfather and I

Go walking in the rain

And thinking.

I can tell that he's remembering.

His face seems softer and so far away.

There's a space between us as we walk,

And though he will not notice it,

I can feel it's always there.

My grandfather and I

Go walking in the rain

And thinking.

He sees his own silent, lonely world,

But when the rain stops and

We're still walking,

Only I can see the rainbow.

February 17, 1970

Dear Twilly,

Spring has to come soon. Hey Messiah, don't you know, "There's a new world coming—coming in peace, coming in joy, coming in love!"

February 26, 1970

Dear Twilly,

Elliot overdosed on heroin last night. How can it be? I just saw him the night before at a party in The Village. I can't believe one of my friends is dead from doing drugs. Where are we all heading?

February 28, 1970

Dear Twilly,

Ha! Your name doesn't fit anymore, Twilly. That is an untouched name. I'm no longer seeing with a dreamy vision.

What is it that I am missing? Where is it? What is the way I really want to be? I am artificial. But what *is* real?

March 4, 1970

Dear Twilly,

We have a very weird Social Studies teacher, Mr. Meade. In the middle of everything last week he says, "I want everyone to write a composition about someone who raised the dignity of mankind."

I like writing about weird topics, so I got a book out of the library on Hasidism and I wrote about a Rabbi Isaac Meir of Ger, a contributor to Hasidism. Today he begins the class by saying that all the papers were garbage except for mine.

He gave me an 'A' and said I was the only one who wrote about someone who genuinely raised the dignity of mankind. I was so shocked. I always thought Mr. Meade didn't like me.

April 3, 1970

ON FRIDAY DO YOU WANT TO GO ON A PROTEST MARCH AND RALLY? PASS ME A NOTE BACK.

FRAN

Maybe, but I'm protesting inside anyway.

WHAT DO YOU MEAN YOU'RE PROTESTING INSIDE ANYWAY? WHERE INSIDE? WHEN?

Each little drop of pain is falling in and overflowing. I can't even feel one singular drop anymore. My whole world is flowing with pain.

THAT IS BEAUTIFUL BUT I'M NOT SURE I UNDERSTAND IT?! DID YOU JUST WRITE THAT? IT'S BEAUTIFUL!

Thank you. But it isn't.

WHY ARE YOU SO DEPRESSED? I KNOW YOU DON'T WANT TO TALK, BUT IF YOU DECIDE TO TALK, YOU CAN ALWAYS TELL ME! WHAT DOES IT MEAN?

I wish I knew and could put it in words.

May 24, 1970

Dear Twilly,

I overheard my mother crying and whispering to my father in their bedroom. She was saying, "Why can't she just accept things like other girls her age? Why can't she be happy? Why can't she be like everyone else?"

I wish I wasn't making my mother cry.

October 2, 1970

Dear Twilly,

Today was Yom Kippur. Last night, I had a dream that I don't understand. But somehow, I feel like in the future I will. I feel like this dream is years ahead of me. It goes like this;

I could hear this boy calling me

in his sweet and liquid tongue

to rise up.

I could see him frown at my clothes and tell me I didn't belong where I was and ask me why I felt the need to hide what was beautiful. I could see him tell me how I always seemed to move in shades of violet. I could see him want to pull me into his mind and show me everything he wanted me to see and then become the way he'd always dreamed I'd be.

I could feel his eyes wandering through my eyes for the

Answer. I could feel his soul stumbling through the darkness for my Reason. I could feel his constant Question running through him, pounding on his brain and destroying everything that had made him. For he could not understand why I did not go with him, why I did not follow my heart and be free.

Then I could hear her calling me

tired and hurt

to come back.

I could see her frown at my clothes and pray that none of the neighbors had seen me. I could see her fold her trembling arms around me and pretend she was still holding her little, frightened child. I could hear her whisper she would take care of me. Then I could see her slowly pull herself away and study me carefully, not wanting to believe. I could see her come straight up to me and laugh into my eyes and tell me I still hadn't changed. Then stepping back, watch the tears gently flow over her eyes and down her softly wrinkled cheeks into her lips that were already crying out the words, "Why don't you follow your heart? Why did you have to change?"

And now I wander the streets

all alone

and with each turn in the road

I am home

But still wandering

I can see them both

so vividly.

Their voices echo.

For how could I explain

to those who have

opened themselves

to me,

expecting me

to enter that it was not I

who was meant to enter.

It was not really me they loved but

their own hearts.

How could I explain to the ones

blocking my path

that I was not their Answer. How could I

explain to those who

stood there so

desperately

that I could not

help them; that although they

were both so sure I fit into

their very different dreams,

I didn't even

have a dream.

And the heart

that they both

begged me to follow

didn't even exist.

It was lost

and found

such a long time ago

in some bottomless box

labelled

"Becoming."

October 18, 1970

Dear Twilly,

Over the weekend I went to a Buddhist Center with Carol, and then last night I went to a Nikirun Shoshu meeting at someone's house. We were all barefoot and they gave everyone beads to chant with. Everyone was chanting the same words over and over again. People stood up and said how when they chanted for something, they got it. I asked what if two people are standing at two different bus stops, both chanting for the bus to arrive at the same moment. I didn't understand the answer. Then everyone put their arms around each other, swaying together and chanting. I hated it. I wanted to get away from them as fast as possible. When I ran out the door, an overly friendly woman with strange blue eyes ran after me for blocks 'till finally I got away and jumped on the first bus I could. They have my phone number and address from the Buddhist Center. I hope they don't come after me.

October 20, 1970

Dear Twilly,

The woman with the blue eyes who was after me at the meeting, so sickeningly friendly, keeps calling me on the phone. I feel really frightened of her. Now I'm leaving the phone off the hook. She called all through last night.

October 25, 1970

With my own two hands and my soul I had made it.

It had silly things like dreams and hope and reaching,

and crazy things like love.

It was made of little bits and Big Enormous Things.

Once I had built it, I went on a search to find other Mountains, but I couldn't find any. So I went back to my Mountain—but I couldn't find it.

All I could find were mountains and mountains

November 11, 1970

Dear Twilly,

Stan Cohen started going to the Christian Science Church near here and he gave me a great book to read about it. There are many beautiful things in it like, "Every listening ear can hear God speak." I think I will start going to the Sunday school classes at the Christian Science Church with him next week.

December 18, 1970

Dear God,

Tonight, with Stan Cohen at the Church, there was music by a man named Larry Gross. I felt like there was an uplifting Presence around us, and we were aware of it. The Presence is always there, but we are not always awake to sense it. There is no need for fear in this real world. What could there possibly be to be afraid of with a totally loving God? God is like a mother hugging all her children. And I am another one of God's perfect children.

Tonight I was with so many good and receptive people. I feel lonely and different from other people so often, but tonight I met so many people like me. Tonight I met some of God's Ideas and I loved them all. There is so much I want to become. And forever to become it.

Just to know there are other people like me is comforting.

Chapter Three: 1971-1973

January 15, 1971

Dear Twilly,

I was afraid to bring you along. What if I would lose you? But luckily I found this hotel stationery in the bureau drawer here, so now I can write to you, Twil. I'm with my parents at a resort hotel up in the Catskills called Kutscher's. We've never gone to a place like this. My parents probably never could have afforded to come to a place like this before now. This is where we've heard a lot of Jewish people come to have a good time. They have swimming pools, saunas, massage parlors, exercise equipment, exercise classes, dance studios, square dancing, skiing, snowmobiles, ice-skating rinks, roller-skating rinks, art auctions, trivia contests, BINGO, and all kinds of entertainment. Everyone stuffs themselves at the smorgasbords at least three times a day with mountains of gefilte fish, matzo balls, knishes, *kashe varnishkes*, *kishkes*, kugels, borscht, pastrami, salami, baloney, chopped liver, corned beef, apple strudel, rugelach *ad nauseum*, not to mention all the bagels and lox. The guests all leave the dining areas complaining that they ate too much, and four hours later they're at it again. Must be all the roller-skating works up a big appetite.

You're supposed to keep having fun every minute here. Twilly, it's unbearable. You're lucky you're not here. My parents don't seem too happy here either. How come it seems so purposeless? I don't understand why people need to be distracted all the time to enjoy themselves. But, distracted from what?

March 8, 1971

walking in the

    cool, damp woods,

I need to

    look at everything.

And share the feeling of becoming alive.

      I like to walk

         in the woods

            and feel so beautiful.

I wonder

    why every soul doesn't long

                   to

wander here,

      in God's woods,

Changing

    to blue

      in a gray world.

March 24, 1971

Dear Twilly,

I love my teacher in the Christian Science Sunday School. She is such a warm, loving person. She is so encouraging, not at all like any of the teachers I used to have in creepy Hebrew School. And I love what I have learned about how God is all-powerful and that when we realize this, as God's children, we have unlimited potential. That changed my whole view of school. Since I've started going to church my grades have shot up from a 78 average to a 98 average! All of a sudden, it is like my head has opened up and I see how I can "plug into" God's infinite potential and just get 100 on every test!

The only thing I don't like about the Christian Science Church is that they keep mentioning Jesus's name. We have to recite certain things from the Bible about him, and I don't want to do that part. For some reason, I get an uneasy feeling in my stomach every time his name is mentioned and I can't bring myself to say it along with everyone else. Why should I feel like this? I actually get very queasy when we're standing and reciting those things and I feel almost like I am going to faint.

May 21, 1971

Dear Twilly,

Why am I always split in two? Why can't I hang out with friends who are smoking and really be there? Why do I have to be home loving my parents? Why can't I cut school and *be there*? Without that other part of me wanting to be in school, being good?

Why do I have to have that other consciousness always following me when I want to have fun?

June 1, 1971

Dear Twilly,

My parents told me today that they want me to go on a teen tour to Israel for the summer. Nobody in my family has ever gone there. I know it's because they want to try to pull me away from Christian Science. But I am *also* really hoping I can get to go.

Application for U.S.Y. Israel Pilgrimage July-August 1971

I would love to go to Israel. Many people would love to go because of a lifelong dream they have had. When they even say the word, "Israel" something pulls strongly inside them. I respect these people greatly. I would love to feel something and believe in something as strongly as they do. I admire these people, but I don't share in their understanding.

I feel, somehow, that Israel could help me. I want to be in the spiritual city of Jerusalem. I want to go to the land where dreams are fulfilled. I feel drawn to Israel like a magnet.

When I was in temple, I saw an old religious man sitting in the back. He was praying with such emotion, such love, that it made my own emotionless state very evident to me. His face was filled with so many years of thought. I want to go to Israel because when I come back and say "Jerusalem" in my prayers, I will really be there, along with the old man in the back.

July 1, 1971

Dear Twilly,

I am here.

I know very strongly inside of me already that Israel and I were made for each other. After we got off the plane, the bus took us straight to Jerusalem, straight to the Wailing Wall and the beautiful night hit me. The Bible actually came alive. It was spectacular.

I felt so guilty for turning away from Judaism last year. I belong to it so much. It's *me*. Just by being here, I feel creativity growing in me already. Touching the Wall touched something in me that is buried deeply, afraid to come out. Can I find deep within me the strength that helps that Wall to keep standing?

I can hardly believe it's for real. The Old City looks like a fairy tale village I've been dreaming about for years.

July 5, 1971

The big why is hitting me in the face.

I am so spoiled.

Today we saw the memorial to the Holocaust

at Yad Va Shem.

And now we are sitting around the dining area,

complaining about the food

and our hotel rooms.

But that photo of the man with *tallis* and *tefillin* praying, surrounded by laughing Nazi soldiers,

keeps staring at me.

How strong his prayers must have been,

With a feeling that even went beyond death,

can we still have that kind of strength?

July 16, 1971

There is still an ember glowing which I have been trying to smother. But it will just keep on glowing, probably sinking deeper and deeper into my being. I don't feel at all safe with it. It is also the free spirit inside of me, which I am trying to hold down with earth-bound chains. It is almost a sacred part of me; too much for me ever to speak about or even think about. It is the Song of Songs of myself.

July 21, 1971

Dear Twilly,

When I am praying

When I am listening and learning

I feel like me.

July 23, 1971

Dear Twilly,

Today, this Saturday morning, I was thrown out of a little Orthodox synagogue in Mea Shearim. It hurt a lot. We were told we had to cover our arms to go there, so I wrapped my crocheted shawl around my shoulders, over my sleeveless dress. All the women there started screaming at me and calling me names in a language I didn't understand. I found out afterwards what they were shouting at me: something like "shameful woman!" And you know what? Suddenly that's what I felt like there. They pushed me out of the synagogue and chased me away,

Could *this* be God's world?

August 13, 1971

Israel

land of hidden hopes and dreams;

dreams to become a little rich America.

Israel

land that is constantly searching

for money.

Israel

land of the chosen people

tourists.

Israel

what happened to your dreams,

your searching, your

people?

Israel

maybe you lost something

in translation?

August 16, 1971

Still,

God is somewhere...

September 9, 1971

I just got glasses.

I can see narrow lines,

precise lettering and make

accurate descriptions.

But now I wish that the moon still had a haze

surrounding it,

and I could always imagine

people were smiling in the streets.

Sometimes I wish I didn't just get glasses.

The world was so much softer then.

February 4, 1972

Dear Twilly,

It's so unbelievably easy to make someone happy. People are embarrassed to show their real feelings. When you give away feelings, you leave yourself open to get hurt. Nobody wants to hurt someone else unless they were hurt themselves by someone.

How come I can't just walk up to a person I love and let them know that I love them?

February 15, 1972

Girls and boys

start again,

playing hide-and-go-seek.

But we are no longer children

and the game has lost all of its joy.

February 27, 1972

Stan

Arming myself in boots and gloves and a coat and umbrella

to go out to meet the wind and snow and ice

makes me wonder,

maybe you also clothe yourself in armor

but in protection

from my warmth.

January 6, 1973

When I am most honest with myself,

I don't pretend I make the sun shine.

I wonder if you would still be my friend,

Once you knew how I was empty.

But,

How could I ever take that chance?

March 11, 1973

Dear Twilly,

They make all the girls take a Home Ec cooking class.
Some nerve! I've been refusing to do any cooking in the
class and I've gotten everyone else to rebel against the
teacher, too. But today she tells me she is going to fail me if

I don't participate and stop instigating everyone. And if you fail this stupid class, you don't graduate. She told me I don't have to do any cooking, but if I would just help set the tables and decorate them and stop instigating everyone, she'll still pass me. I guess I'll do that, but it just bugs me that the boys don't have to take cooking, and I have to study something that is not relevant to my future life. I want to be a scientist.

May 7, 1973

Sometimes I think that girls can never be free.

Perhaps they weren't meant to be.

The boys ran down the mountain, faster and faster as they grew.

But when the girls grew,

their running faltered.

August 10, 1973

Dear Twilly,

I just finished reading my *Seventeen* magazine. Soon I'll switch my subscription to *Glamour*. Then I guess I'm supposed to gradually move up to *Ladies Home Journal* or *Good Housekeeping*.

On one page there was an article, "Count Your Calories! Diet Tips from the Experts" A few pages later, there's a glossy photo of a double-layer chocolate velvet cake with huge globs of whipped cream on top. This was followed by several pages of recipes entitled: "Indulge!" Then there was an ad for super sheer panty hose worn by a super skinny model. Next a lipstick ad, "Exercises for the Tummy!" and "Go Italian: Have a Lasagna Party Tonight" Then came another skinny model offering appetite depressant sucking candies. God, I'm confused. Am I supposed to be skinny or eat?

October 14, 1973

Over forty young women packed into a small, dimly-lit room in the basement of Forest Hills High School today. Everyone sat cross-legged on the floor. Our first "Women's Forum" meeting took place today and I couldn't believe so many women showed up. All I did was put up a few posters. But the time is right. The views expressed by radical feminists years back have seeped down into the minds of young women like us, in high schools across the nation. We are now questioning the traditional woman's role in our future. I was nervous to get up and speak in front of everybody, but also much too happy to care.

This is what I said: "First, I want to thank everyone for coming. It is very important that women get together to share ideas and goals and problems. Just by getting together we become stronger. Later on at this meeting, I'd like to talk about some important changes that we could work on right here in our high school. Like getting girls, I should say, women, to be allowed to take 'shop' classes here like woodworking and drafting and printing. But I want to begin now by reading you a story I have just written which I think expresses fears that many of us have. Afterwards, I'd like to hear your comments and questions; what you all think about my essay. It is called:

"A Dollhouse Reality"

When a little girl receives her first miniature kit of make-up, her first Little Miss Happy Homemaker ironing board set, or her first Betsy Wetsy doll, she does not realize the huge price that she will eventually have to pay for them. She can hardly wait for the day when those plastic playthings will become their real selves, and she will be able to spend her mornings to evenings involved in an endlessly long game of playing house.

All that the little girl ever dreams about is one perfectly wonderful day. The day of the pure white lace gown, surrounded by plenty of admirers, and topped with one single, eternal promise; that alluring promise of contentment.

Ever since the day when a certain little girl felt the eyes of a certain little boy shyly looking at her from across her fourth grade classroom, and she couldn't stop herself from blushing furiously, she knew she wouldn't ever be the same. She had just been caught up into something much larger than herself and she would never again be free.

Suddenly her mad passion for secret clubhouse meetings, treasure-hunting expeditions, and squirrel chasing would be put aside forever. Bill, in fourth grade, Jeff, in fifth grade, Gregg, in sixth grade, and all the others until Mike, in college, would become her main objectives. The contest got uglier as the years went on. At first it was new and innocent enough, but over the years it got more desperate. The goal was to get the best prize of all, a cute and successful one. It was generally accepted that the girl who came in last would get the booby prize. Those who never made it to the finish line had to pick up all the scattered pieces of confetti strewn around, after the winners had passed by. Nobody wanted to be left in that lonely and degrading position, so everyone kept running in the race as fast as they could.

Along the way, the little girl would learn a lot of helpful hints. She would learn how to apply make-up skillfully in order to cover up her inner beauty. She would learn how to be charming and irresistible and how to hide her true personality. She would learn that the most important thing in life is to catch a great guy, even if that means sacrificing herself in the process. She would learn her lessons very easily, without much effort. Because all around her would be advertisements, movies, parents, and pals pointing out the road that would lead her to guaranteed happiness.

If she failed to learn her lessons well, she would be laughed at and ostracized. She would get her most important education from billboard posters or have to live with the terrible pain of being alone. If she was smarter than she was supposed to be, or if she preferred to play basketball on weekends, she could never attain the contentment that all the others would be able to achieve. She would be made to suffer for not losing what they had all lost years before.

When a little girl finally does receive her long-pursued playthings, lo and behold, they somehow don't manage to bring the same kind of happiness that they did when they were only toys. An ironing board now means piles of wrinkled laundry, which means dreary, boring afternoons without ever feeling the sunshine. Betsy Wetsy is still a joy to the little girl grown older. But now, to her surprise, the life-size doll has an endless list of needs and demands that can only be met by her mother, day in and day out.

The little girl is no longer a little girl, and she wonders where her life has gone. It has been a long time since she has done something she could feel proud of. Now she is like a machine, a spiritless body that gets up each day and goes through the motions of being alive. She feels hardly any emotions anymore, except for a dull pain that goes through and through her.

Sometimes it's hard to smile with the children, and so she screams at them and blames them for her unhappiness. Sometimes she's angry at her husband for chaining her down into this deadening life. At first she stops doing little, barely noticeable things, like baking her special cakes for the family or organizing weekend picnics. Then she stops trying futilely to hold onto her waning beauty. And as she stops, she starts slowly falling apart. She begins to cry silently whenever they're not watching and she starts wondering more and more often how she got deceived; cheated into believing in The Great Lie.

The little girl, no longer a little girl, realizes that the contentment she was always striving to obtain was just a mirage that vanished mysteriously when she got to it. It was all just a dream that had been created to give some meaning to their lives. But actually, it had taken out all the meaning that was once growing deep inside.

But it's too late now. Squirrels aren't running by, treasure-hunting has lost its original appeal, and by now her own little Betsy Wetsy has grown up. She's reading magazines that have catchy little phrases like, "A Diamond is Forever," smeared all over them.

October 20, 1973

Dear Twilly,

Ever since I lost fifteen pounds, Stan has looked at me in a whole different way. Once I really wished I could be his girlfriend. But I gave up years ago, and I grew to love our special friendship. And now, after all these years of being such great friends, he suddenly wants me as a girlfriend. I love playing guitar and writing songs together, and most of all, sharing inner feelings. But I really don't want all this other stuff that he wants. I'm so confused about which way to go. I don't want to lose his friendship.

November 27, 1973

"Rabbi Darby, Cantor Lowy, members of the Sisterhood and Men's Club, and all the congregants present here at the Rego Park Jewish Center's Friday Night Kiddush tonight, thank you for allowing me to speak to you. I believe that a re-evaluation of the woman's role in Judaism today is necessary since a giant step forward is about to be taken. This June, Sally Preisand will be ordained as the first woman rabbi in Jewish history. To me, this event testifies to the fact that Judaism is still a living religion.

I think it is important to understand fully that Sally Preisand's goal is not to lessen the significance of any Jewish traditions, but only to add to their beauty and sacredness. It is only a symbolic move, however. The true restrictions still remain in place, in our own self-made, limiting sense of values. The derogatory image of the stereotypic Jewish American woman as being nothing but a "yenta" needs to be totally destroyed.

I can't understand why there should be any objection to opening up a source left untapped far too long. It is a source that is filled with creative ideas, rich insight and unlimited benefits for every aspect of Judaism. Why is it that on the Board of Trustees in our Conservative Jewish Center, out of about thirty members only two are women and only one of those two women has the right to vote in this synagogue's elections? And why do women so rarely address the congregation from the pulpit?

Part of the problem is that there is still far less emphasis placed on educating a Jewish girl than there is on educating a Jewish boy. *Veshi'nantam le vanecha,* "And you shall teach to your children" from our Shema is addressed to *both* sexes.

We should intensify the encouragement of education for Jewish girls, but we cannot do that unless we get rid of some limitations in our minds. Times have changed. It is now understood that women do have the same intellectual, emotional, and spiritual ability as men. We *have* come this far. We must now make of ourselves the new image that so many Jewish women now desperately need.

A woman is almost entirely responsible for the future morality of the coming generation. After all, the Talmud does admit, "When you educate a man, you educate a man; educate a woman, and you educate a family."

Chapter Four: 1974

Application to Radcliffe College/Harvard University

Part IV: Essay Section

I have faith in the human potential. I believe that each individual can grow and develop without ever having to fix upon himself restrictive and erroneous limitations. Each person has the ability to experience life in a degree so much greater than the level at which he usually permits himself to remain.

Each person has so many avenues open to him that are either never uncovered or lie weeded over from disuse. I love to learn, to reach out and discover all that there is to know about the world. I love to watch all the changes that take place as I grow because they are indications to me of how much I am alive.

After school hours, I have a volunteer job working at the Forest View Nursing home in Forest Hills, Queens. I help feed and visit the patients in their rooms. My favorite activity of all, however, is working in the Recreation Department, doing crafts with the patients. I made up a project in which the patients make toys—stuffed animals, puppets, mobiles—for an orphanage nearby.

Now the patients know that they are doing something very useful, not just "busywork." Their colorful, lively products are proof that they are talented individuals who had simply been convinced that they were nothing more than bothersome beings, taking up needed space.

It is not enough to keep people alive as long as possible. When they have nothing to live for, no one that needs them, and no hope for themselves, are they really living? Some of my elderly friends have realized that they *are* still valuable human beings. And that has changed them. To me, being alive means that there is always a chance to grow.

April 8, 1974

I can't believe this is happening. My parents thought I should just apply to the state schools in New York, but my college guidance counselor suggested I give the Ivy-League schools a try, and so I did.

And right away Harvard, Yale, and Princeton all sent me back "Early Evaluations" saying that they were happy to inform me that I'm at the top of the pool of applicants that they want to accept! Even my college guidance counselor was shocked. And then the phone-calls started. Alumnae and Admissions Officers from Harvard, Yale, and Princeton keep calling me up, trying to convince *me* to choose *their* university! I just can't understand why they all want me. Someone told me that they've got this formula all worked out in the Ivy-League Admissions Offices. Just from reading each application, they pretty much know which applicants will become big successes later on in life and those are the people they really go after.

How come everything suddenly feels like it's coming too fast and too easily?

April 27, 1974

I wish so much I was just a baby. I don't want to think; not about tomorrow or the day after that. Oh please God, let me not think. God, if I only believed in you. If I only believed in something. Please God, let me stop thinking. My parents seem so very far away now. Nobody can come close. I want someone to come in, but I don't want anyone to. I want to be alone. But God, please don't let me be alone.

I don't want to grow up. I hate thinking. Why was I made to do it so much? Up until now, I could just slide along, following the directions. Now it's on my own. Now it's my own mistakes. Now I get a chance to screw up my own life like everyone else does. I want to stop thinking. But I can't. Shut up brain. Sometimes I try so hard not to be different. I don't want to be. Sometimes I wish I was stupid and happy. Why isn't that good enough for me?

I am so worried about college. Next year seems so frightening. God, I don't want to grow up. I can't even think of one good way my life could possibly take me. There is nothing I really want in life. It all seems so pointless.

I know that maybe even by tomorrow, I'll be back to the normal way of acting. I'll get right into the swing of things again. I won't even be able to tell me apart. But right now, even the thought of escaping into that shallow level of living makes me sick. Oh God, I can't even think of anything to wish for. Just to stop thinking.

May 8, 1974

I'm probably the only person who rebelled against their parents by going to Harvard. Princeton seemed so tame and refined (boring) when I went there with my parents to check out what it was like. They wanted me to go there.

But then we took a train to Boston and the subway to

Harvard Square, and when we got out of the subway station, the first sight we stared at was a bunch of drug addicts lying around on the street of the Square. To me, the whole scene just looked like such a fun, exciting hippie kind of place. I started squealing, "Me! This place is me!" My parents were just giving each other looks.

When we got back to New York, the first chance I had when my parents weren't home, I checked off the little box on the return card I received in my "acceptance envelope" saying that, yes, I wanted to attend Radcliffe/Harvard. Then I ran out to the mailbox and mailed the return form immediately. When my parents came home, I told them what I had done, with a wicked grin. Cambridge, here I come!

May 14, 1974

I keep having the same dream. I'm brushing my teeth, talking on the phone, or even trying to do math homework, and it comes back to me. It's haunting me and I want to get rid of it. I keep dreaming my life as a total failure. I can't ever stop this dream from coming back.

In the dream, I am crouched in the street by the gutter. Nothing looks familiar, and yet everything resembles something that I know. I've been there so many times before, but I don't remember ever really coming near those dingy streets. God, how I pray I never will. Please God, don't make me go on alone. I'm not ready. How will I know which way to turn? I just know I'll end up there. Please give me some kind of directions, so I'll have some idea of which way I should go. I want to go the right way. But I can't possibly get there alone.

There's something wrong with the place. There is

everything wrong with it. But there's something in particular that I want to keep away from. Will I learn to fly when I go away or always walk on a boring, straight path? Don't let me fly too high. That's what I'm afraid of. How will I know when to glide down gently? Nobody's told me how high is too high.

The streets there are all frightening. They are filled with lost, empty people, with burning eyes. They are all searching frantically for something. But their eyes won't rest on me. They don't even see me. Their eyes search right through me and past me as if I was never there. Please God, please let them see me.

But I don't want people now. I don't want to get too used to being loved. Wearing a winter coat indoors and then going outside makes it seem even colder. I want someone to hug me now so much that it hurts. But no one should come near me. I need to be alone. To let my dreams come back into me and describe my failure more clearly.

I am letting some parts of me usually kept under wraps fly out, but I don't really trust them. I can't leave them alone, without supervision. There is that part of me which will never come home at night. Please let it come home. And rest, sometimes. Let those parts be careful, of me.

Sometimes the different parts in me seem like in Joseph's dreams, one part completely devouring the other. Please God, please let them all live together.

I want to be strong. But how will I be able to love myself when no one else is there to? I don't have enough stored up inside to go on without refueling. Someone please help me believe that I'll be strong enough.

The dream is filled with people hurrying quickly by me. The pervasive feeling is loneliness. Each time I dream it, I get more and more frightened. I want to say that I need somebody, but I can never ask anyone to help me. I feel like the fear is crawling through the warm and sturdy structures within me, and eroding them. But I can never admit to anyone the failure dream that keeps coming back to me. I wish it would go away. But it won't. It's waiting until I do.

July 29, 1974

This summer I have a job working as a check-out girl at Key Food Supermarket. I love it. I am acting the whole time. Joking. I even pull my hair back in a pony-tail and chew gum all the time to look the part. I love pretending I am nothing but a check-out girl. Nobody there knows I am going to Radcliffe in a few weeks.

It's kind of sad, though, that to the other check-out girls this is probably all there is. This is their whole life.

There's something that seems even sadder to me, though. I can't stop thinking about how all the people work to buy their food (which I check out) to live another day to work to buy their food (which I check out) to live another day to work to…

It's scary. Am I inside of an even bigger joke? Is this really all there is *for every one of us*?

August 28, 1974

Dear Twilly (for old time's sake),

It is the night before leaving for Harvard, and I feel like I want to die.

Why bother acting out all the scenes I have already written? I know how it will all turn out. Tomorrow I'll be going to

Harvard, majoring in psychology and taking pre-med requirements. After graduation, I'll go to medical school and become a psychiatrist. Somewhere along the line, I will get married and have two kids. He'll be something like an architect and we'll live in a big house near the coast in California. Why not die right now and avoid wasting all that time going through with the whole scenario?

It seems so meaningless. True, the husband and the children I'll have and all the other people I'll care about will add color and warmth to the picture, but still...

Every dream I ever had has come true already. What more is there to reach for? At graduation I skipped up to the stage, picking up awards in almost every subject. I can still hear all that delicious applause from the thousands of people filling the huge auditorium. I pretended to take it all in modestly. I'll be re-running that whole scene for decades to come.

The day that was the absolute tops, though, was the day I ripped open the envelope this spring, telling me that because of the scores I got on the various Achievement tests I took, I had gotten into Harvard with Sophomore Standing. I could enter Harvard, skipping my freshman year! But *now*, what do I have to look forward to? Tomorrow my parents will be driving me up to Harvard, and they'll leave me there. With a whole school full of other Wonder Boys and Girls. All with planned-out dreams like mine, already mostly completed.

But when I was twelve, and going through a lot of changes, wasn't there a routine I made up that showed me I really did want to be alive? Remember, Twilly? Whenever I was feeling things strongly at night, I'd lock the door to my room, throw open the window, and stick myself out. But not too far, because if nothing else, I liked repeating the whole routine.

I would lean out until only my waist was on top of the window sill and my feet were dangling in the air. From my third-story window, when I leaned out far like that, I could see all the cars going by on Queens Boulevard and think, *There is at least one person in each of those cars. There are hundreds of people driving by. There are billions of people in the world. I'm just one of them.* I'd start to feel a sort of unity between all those unknown people driving out there and me. They all had problems and each of their problems seemed like the whole universe to them. Each in their own world, they didn't even know that they were driving through mine.

Was each car driving by so I could see it at this moment? Was there some Plan to all this? Why? *Why* was life worth living? I'd look straight down to the pavement below and think how all I had to do was let go and that would be it. Only then would I become aware of my fingers and how desperately they were clutching onto that ledge.

I am going to get up and do that old routine right now.

Twilly, you still there? *Me too!* I was hanging way out the ol' window, and just as I barely started to lose my balance, those trusty fingers grasped onto the ledge just as tightly as ever. I really *do* want to live! And while hanging out there, I remembered one more step in my favorite routine: feeling the night air.

On my arms, on my cheeks, and eyelashes, whether winter or summer, night air always gives me a chill. The Tree that I used to talk to outside my window was cut down years ago. But when I closed my eyes this time, I still shivered from the breeze that once went through its branches. My deepest questions about the purpose of life are left unanswered. But the night air, blowing softly through my hair, is enough for right now.

Journal

October 14, 1974

Now I am at Harvard and I'm 18, too old for a diary. So I'll call it a journal.

I've got to get this all down on paper. I met this guy on the shuttle bus and he asked me to go out with him. He is pure blonde WASP and he thinks I'm exotic and interesting *because* I'm Jewish.

I'm afraid to say much when I'm with him because it might not be interesting. I want to keep up the exotic image, so when I absolutely have to speak, I talk in a whisper. He's twenty-five. It's so exciting. I'm just afraid that I'm playing a part in a movie that is going to end soon.

November 11, 1974

The movie's over. Paul told me he had been attracted to me at first because he thought there was so much to me, but then I almost never said anything. And most of all, he couldn't stand how, when I did say something, I always talked in a whisper that started to really get on his nerves.

November 15, 1974

There was a yellow rose scotch-taped on my door today when I got back from buying posters in the Coop. And there was a little note scotch-taped to the rose which just said, "Love, Michael." That's a guy who lives down the hall here in the dorm. I never really thought much about him before.

He's a sophomore; a math and philosophy major, I think. I think that's all I know about him. Guess I'll get to know him better.

Chapter Five: 1975

February 12, 1975

We all sit around here in the dining hall for hours—over breakfast, over lunch, over dinner, over late-night coffee—discussing life. And nobody talks about feelings here. Only ideas. We're always analyzing, analyzing, analyzing, but none of us wants to get up and do anything besides re-fill our own coffee mugs. I'm getting the hang of this.

May 11, 1975

Two nights ago, Michael went to visit an old girlfriend. I must have gained twenty pounds that night at the all-night grill. But when he finally returned, he was so nice to me again. You can't trust men. You can't open your heart to them. They're flighty.

September 10, 1975

That good ol' shuttle bus ride back to Radcliffe from Harvard Square... All the people huddled together in the rain. Everyone wet and tired, but very beautiful. Eating a warm blueberry muffin in a favorite tucked-away coffeehouse in the Square. It's been such a great welcome back!

I decorated my dorm room like the dream room I always wanted as a kid! I bought a hobby horse, *just like* they had on Romper Room. And I bought big sheets of colored cardboard and made a playhouse in the middle of the room, exactly the way I always wanted to make one. I drew windows and a door on it and everything. And I can go inside it and pretend! And I got this quilted granny doll and she sits in a child-sized rocking chair that I can just barely squeeze into. I bought the chair and the doll in this great second-hand shop and I put them in the window corner of my room.

And now today, the finishing touch! I went out and collected a whole bunch of authentic New England Autumn leaves! Orange, red, brown, and every shade of gold! Then I mounted my very favorite ones on waxed paper and made "leaf people" out of them, just like I used to do when I was younger. Now I have leaf people hung up all over the walls of my room. And I taped the most beautiful ones up on the windows, next to the Wandering Jew plant hanging there. I brought the Wandering Jew with me from home. Oh, my room is *fantastic*!

October 8, 1975

I was with Michael last night, when I felt his eyes studying me. Then he suddenly said, "You know, I really like thinner types."

He said it in such a cool, detached way you'd think he was talking about some philosophical argument. We had a big fight after that. He doesn't even *understand* why I am hurt! But the pain of that moment—standing there feeling rejected—will it ever go away?

October 12, 1975

I wear black now every day. Black Levis and a black B.V.D. T-shirt. Does it look like I'm in mourning? I don't care. It makes me look a lot thinner.

I miss Michael terribly. I am still hoping, daydreaming about how I'll come back to my room and there will be a note on my door saying something like: "I didn't mean what I said at all," and he'll be there, waiting for me.

November 23, 1975

Michael came back. But during the time we were apart, I've been feeling that there is something more. Yes, something even more encompassing, that goes even deeper. I've been reading a lot of Hasidic tales. These tales make me feel that there is more, and I know it even when I'm not facing it. There is something peaceful—something that transcends even this—and I can sense it just a little.

November 30, 1975

Love can be a spiritual feeling. When I walked into a dark temple all alone one day years back I had a small sense of this feeling. Scary, but incredibly exciting—this ultimate kind of union.

Individual connections can take place with anyone and anything, but our "attachments" make it easier for us to make a connection with particular qualities. But it doesn't have to be this way. With the fixed Hasidic marriages, deep connections could be achieved, too, I bet. If each person does not fight against his energy and lets it flow naturally, deep, lasting unions can be made.

December 1, 1975 morning

An important point, that seems to strike right to the center of things, I read about today in the credos of Hasidism. "He who speaks of worldly matters and religious matters as if they were separate and distinct is a heretic." I always do that, but sometimes they do feel intertwined.

December 3, 1975

I figured out the secret to getting "A's" here. Write papers relating things to each other; show I see how *everything's* relative. That's the *truth* we're supposed to learn at Harvard. That's what the *Ve ri tas* on the Harvard insignia must mean! Inscribed on every Harvard pen, Harvard mug, Harvard sweatshirt, so we'll inscribe it in our hearts!

December 18, 1975

I'm very tense about going home to my parents for Christmas Break. But I know I do have to face them, and not run away from what's going on. I have to integrate all the different parts in me.

December 21, 1975

Home now. They are making constant references to Michael's being Catholic. It must touch some guilt spot within me, too. I guess I really don't feel as easy about it as I thought. Judaism is important to me, but I still feel that an issue like this seems superfluous to our relationship.

Making a fuss about it doesn't demonstrate the strength of one's feelings for Judaism. Do I have to declare out loud that Judaism *is* an essential part of me for someone to believe me? But I do not see any conflict just because Michael and I are from different religions. I don't think I can explain it to my parents. But I don't want to toss them off like they can't understand. Why are they making everything so complicated?

December 22, 1975

There have been almost constant arguments going on here about Michael's not being Jewish. It's like a wall that is always there now between me and my parents. But there's no reason for it to be there. I mean, what's the big deal? Didn't they bring me up to be liberal-minded and love all kinds of people?

December 28, 1975

I've been avoiding writing. But what am I really trying to avoid? I've spent the past few days with Michael's family. Michael has three brothers and five sisters and such wonderful, loving parents. I've always dreamed of being part of a big family like this. There is always so much activity going on here. There's something happening in every room in this big, fun, rambling house. I loved Christmas here so much. I felt like I fit right in.

Except for when we all went to Midnight Mass. I just couldn't get myself to kneel down in that huge church. I don't know why. It seemed like there were thousands of people there and I was the only one standing up. I felt so strange.

My mother sounded very hurt on the phone that I wasn't home to light the Chanukah candles with them this year. But I've always wanted to experience Christmas. Today, we went sleigh-riding down the big hill in their backyard. I *love* it here.

December 29, 1975

So many different feelings. Everything suddenly seems as far away from simple as I can imagine. I just feel like running. But to where?

The furniture is being moved around in my head upstairs. Things are being re-arranged. And there's a lot of confusion as to where things should be placed.

I always find it necessary to report happy things like achievements and accomplishments, as if I've really *made them*. As if I've brought them about through all my work, through my own power. Am I moving things around? Or, am I being moved around? I am making choices. But it is so confusing to know what to choose.

Chapter Six: 1976

January 4, 1976

Back at home. Tonight a friend called me up who I had not spoken to in seven years. She was my friend in camp when we both began to ask basic questions about life. The two of us had feelings that seemed so different than everyone else there. She had been going through old stuff and found some things we had written to each other back then. The thoughts and feelings we expressed then were so clear, as if they came directly out from our inner selves, nothing mangling them in the process. Just spilling out exactly the way we felt them. If only everything was still filled with all the wonder we perceived then.

January 12, 1976

I returned to Harvard today after Christmas break. I went wandering through Widener Library in the afternoon and I found this book of Hasidic tales that someone left out on a table:

"A young rabbi complained to the Rabbi of Rizhyn: 'During the hours when I devote myself to my studies I feel life and light, but the moment I stop studying it is all gone. What shall I do?'

The Rabbi of Rizhyn replied: 'That is just as when a man walks through the woods on a dark night, and for a time another joins him, lantern in hand, but at the crossroads they part and the first must grope his way on alone. But if a man carries his own light with him, he need not be afraid of any darkness.'"

Whose embrace am I *really* seeking?

Michael took off this term. He got a leave of absence from school. He's living in New York City, trying to determine what he wants to do with his life. He left Harvard in order to be able to make some clear decisions. It's difficult to have the strength to leave here. I've been making some new friends, too, like Steve and Leah, which is nice.

Walking alone feels very different now. I do not feel alone. Almost all the leaves are gone now, but really, aren't they scattered all over the world?

March 12, 1976

I've been taking a lot of walks lately, looking around like a four-year-old first discovering spring. It's always surprising to see what pops up in the world. It feels good to be moving on my own.

And it's very strange the way people are, the way we *do* seem to know things going on beneath the surface. Even when we're not even aware of them.

March 28, 1976

I tried going to the Harvard Hillel again, the Jewish organization on campus. There was an "Oneg Shabbos" talk. I hated it. They never talk about anything spiritual. It's always some political issue. Why do I waste my time going, hoping that this time it will be different? Hoping for those Hasidic Rabbis of the past that I read about to still be alive, just waiting to talk to me about all of my questions. Like I love the idea of Shabbos. It's so me. But I know I would never keep it by myself.

April 11, 1976

I do volunteer work at Westborough State Hospital. It's a mental hospital, a forty minute drive from Harvard. It's a very scary place. I go there in a van twice a week with two other students. We are working on an experimental program to train "the most promising" mental patients to become outpatients. They won't be going back to their families, though, but to apartments with their fellow patients in this program.

Today they just told me that one of the patients I talk to a lot—he is the one I can really relate to the most—was once also a student at Harvard. Did that petrify me! I guess that's because here I am, having just been nominated to Phi Beta Kappa at Harvard, and here he is, having just been nominated to become an outpatient at Westborough State. And he was once where I was. That's not what scares me. It's that I know there is really such a very thin line separating us. It's that I know we could so easily switch places.

May 27, 1976

In my Psych and Soc Rel Tutorial, I did my term paper on obesity and anorexia. I learned a tremendous amount doing research into the field of eating disorders. People are always asking me why I picked this subject to go into in depth when I'm not anorectic or obese. I'm not really sure why. It just interests me a lot.

Also, I was in a great seminar this term, "Biology and Women's Issues." And for this class, too, I wrote my paper about anorexia. It was called, "Why Are So Many Anorexics Women?" I loved the instructor of the course, but I felt kind of intimidated by the other students in the seminar. They seemed angry. I'm also a feminist, but how come I'm not angry like them?

And I always feel like I have to hide Michael's existence. Like he's from enemy territory. *Now* it's some kind of sin to *have* a boyfriend!

I feel so often when I am with these other women that there is something I want to stand up and tell them. But I have no idea what it is.

Yesterday the instructor asked me to help her and two other students in the seminar, Barbara and Mary Sue, edit a book. It will be a collection of the papers we wrote for the course!

From:

Women Look at Biology Looking at Women:

A Collection of Feminist Critiques

Why Are So Many Anorexics Women?

It is the first of the month, and on thousands of newsstands across the country, we see the new month's wares. In these enlightened times, some women show signs of resentment as they pass by, casually glancing at the covers of popular "women's" magazines that line the shelves. Yet even many women who understand the damage done us by articles like "Do Your Hair and Make-up Like Our Cover Girl and Dazzle Him," still linger hopefully over "Complete Diet Guide For Women On The Go" and "13 Marvelous Diets That Really Work."

It is the first of the month, and millions of women across the country are being fooled into believing that they have weight control problems to which answers are available for fifty cents at any newsstand. A great deal of time and *man*power have been invested to convince women that we have eating disorders whose solutions have finally been discovered. While we have become generally more aware and wary of the "suggestions" offered by the media concerning our life-styles, the advertisements aimed at women with eating control problems have grown more influential. They are effective because they address an area which we have long been pressed not to explore deeply. It is difficult to stop hoping that "maybe this time it will be different, maybe this time one of the thirteen marvelous diets will actually work." Yet it is essential that we give up wishing, and instead begin to ask why women place so much emphasis on body weight.

Let us be clear: the usual weight loss techniques are harmful, no matter what the outcome. If a woman tries to implement one of the "easy" methods and fails, every effort is made to assure her that it is *her* fault, not the methods. And if she succeeds, her "success" story, no matter how short-lived, is publicized not only to obtain more customers, but also to serve as a deterrent to her further understanding of whether she, in fact, *has* a "weight problem," and, if so, why. Only if we address the social context surrounding the issue of our "weight anxiety," instead of manipulating our bodies to conform to the parameters of newsstand beauty, can we hope for a lasting solution to the eating disorders that afflict many women.

Although most popular attention has been directed at "overeating" and "overweight" individuals, it is useful to look at the other extreme, self-starvation or anorexia nervosa. We will then gain some insight into what may motivate some women to use extreme forms of "body language…"

Anorexia has been described as "self-inflicted starvation in the absence of recognizable organic disease and in the midst of ample food." It occurs mostly in young, upper-middle-class white women for whom thinness is a prerequisite for social status, and appears to be on the rise in extremely weight-conscious societies like our own. It is usually observed in young women between the ages of eleven and thirty-five. Approximately ninety-five percent of all anorexics are female…

It is significant that in anorectic women the "much admired feminine curves" are obliterated. One opinion that is therefore prevalent among researchers is that anorexia is "a way to remain physically a child." *Why*, one is prompted to ask, should so many more women than men in our society *want* physically to remain children? Does this suggest that many women so dislike being regarded, first and foremost, as sexual creatures that they prefer to regain a "child-like" shape? If so, anorexia is not a personal neurosis. It reflects an accurate perception of the realities of many women's lives in our society…

July 15, 1976

I started taking a summer course in organic chemistry at NYU so I wouldn't have to take it with all the cut-throat pre-meds at Harvard next year. I took chemistry at NYU last summer and it was great. But I don't know why, I don't have the energy to go for another summer of studying without a break. I can't really concentrate and I failed the first two quizzes they've given so far. I don't really know why. I probably just need a break. I guess I'm going to have to drop out of the course and take it at Harvard next year, after all. I really want to just spend the summer at Michael's family's beach house.

July 18, 1976

It's so relaxing out here with Michael's family. I love this old beach house, waking up every morning with sea breezes blowing in through the curtains. I took a book of Hasidic tales out here with me. Each day I want to try and copy down one of my favorites.

"Rabbi Haim of Volozhin taught: In truth, all the secrets and mysteries of the *Torah* are really perfectly explicit and revealed. It is only that our eyes are covered and we do not see…The fact is that man is often struck by blindness. If a man involves himself in the study of the *Torah* without any thought of self, God will open his eyes and remove the mask of blindness."

July 20, 1976

I love sitting here by the ocean in the late afternoon and writing in this journal. I love Michael's family so much. This is like a dream family to me, all these sisters and brothers. The kind I've only read about in books; a big old-fashioned family. Because my sister, Nancy, is nine years older than me and went off to college when I was only eight, I've felt so often like an only child. I love pretending here that I'm a part of Michael's family.

July 31, 1976

Since Michael is the oldest of all his sisters and brothers, when his parents have to go someplace, we get to take over and watch the whole crew. It is so wonderful playing house. You know, I really think this is all I want in life, being at home with people I care about, cleaning a bit, playing around in the kitchen, doing creative things. Why am I doing this whole pre-med thing anyway? I hate the pressure. I love this simple life so much. But I don't really see how there's a way out of it all. I mean, in this day and age, a person like me has to have some kind of prestigious career. There's no way someone like me can become just a housewife.

"Rabbi Nahman taught: The negative impulse in man is like someone who runs amongst people with his hand closed, and nobody knows what is in it. He tricks people and asks each one: 'What am I holding?' And each person assumes that the closed hand holds something he desires very much. So everyone runs after him. Eventually he opens his hand and there is nothing there at all."

August 9, 1976

My sister and her husband invited Michael and me to come down to Maryland for a few days and stay with them. Nancy arranged for us to have an appointment with the Reconstructionist rabbi at the Hillel of the college where my brother-in-law teaches. She said this rabbi was a great guy that all the college students love. And Michael was even more interested in going than I was. He's even been going with me to the library in town lately and taking out some books on Judaism. I think he knows more about Judaism than I do already.

So we went to this rabbi and I asked him a question I've wanted to ask a rabbi for a long time. "Can I still be a Jew if

I don't believe in God?" For one split second I stood there, so terrified of the answer. And then he said so easily, "Sure. That's what Reconstructionist Judaism is all about. You don't have to believe in God." Michael asked him several questions about Judaism, too. He was very nice to both of us, and when we got back to my sister's house, I told her that her "plan" had backfired. I told her she and our parents didn't have to be upset anymore about Michael's not being Jewish; we had the rabbi's approval.

"Someone once asked the Baal Shem Tov why it was that sometimes when a man cleaves to the Creator, in the very middle of his cleaving, he finds himself suddenly very distant from God.

The Baal Shem Tov answered him with a parable: 'When a father wants to teach his son to walk, what does he do? He takes his son and stands him on the ground in front of him, puts his hands out on either side so that the child does not fall, and the child walks between his father's hands. When the child comes close to where his father is standing, the father withdraws a little so that the child will come on further and further. Thus the child learns how to walk.

'So it is with God. When a man burns with religious fervor and cleaves to God, he withdraws from him, so that a man learns how to strengthen himself more and more in his cleaving to the Divine.'"

August 14, 1976

Michael wanted me to meet his priest. This priest was his favorite teacher in the Jesuit high school Michael had gone to, and Michael still feels very close to him. Father McNally was an incredible person, so insightful and full of sparkling energy. And he said such a strange and interesting thing as we were leaving him. He said, "Michael, it makes so much sense that you are with Joanne. Only a Jewish soul like hers could run deep enough for yours." I don't think I understand what that means. But I like it.

August 17, 1976

A government official asked Rabbi Schneur Zalman of Liadi what it means when it says in the Bible that God called Adam and asked him: 'Where are you?' How could God not have known where Adam was?

The Rabbi replied: 'Do you believe that the Scriptures are of eternal validity, and they exist for each age, each generation, and each man?'

'Yes,' said the official.

The Rabbi continued, 'The verse in Genesis where God calls Adam means that in every age God calls to each man and says to him, 'Where are you? Where are you in this world?'

August 20, 1976

I am so sad to have this beautiful summer ending. Now back to "real life." At least Michael will be returning to Harvard this fall, too. I got pretty tan this summer…and thinner, too!

This is what I read in my Hasidic tales book today: "When a person tastes something, the Baal Shem Tov taught, he should perceive with his understanding that the good within food and drink is nothing other than God Himself, from whom all pleasures derive."

September 15, 1976

Back again for my last year here at Harvard. My advisor couldn't believe that all I plan to take this year is organic chemistry and a course on Soviet films. But I took so many courses during my other two years at Harvard, that I've fulfilled all the requirements already. I'm taking a lot of dance classes in the afternoons and some evenings. And my brain just needs a break. Something in me feels very tired.

October 3, 1976

I have to decide whether I'm going to do a senior thesis or not. Since the grades from my first two years here were in the highest rank group, if I do a thesis, I could graduate from Harvard, *summa cum laude*. But I don't think I can do it. I just can't bring myself to get any more deeply involved with all this eating disorder research, my specialty. I'd like to stop concentrating on it so much. I want to get it out of my thoughts a little.

October 15, 1976

I was asked to give a talk on the research I've done on anorexia. Ever since I gave that lecture to interested students and faculty members, there is this emaciated anorectic/bulimic, Lois Bloomberg, who keeps following me around. She even seeks me out in the dining hall, asking me questions about anorexia, all the while eating piles and piles of food and looking greener by the minute. I know after each of these binge meals, she is going to her room and throwing it all up. I can't stand being with her. She makes me so nervous. I'm shaking after being with her. I've stopped eating my meals in the dining hall now because I don't want to have to see her.

Chapter Seven: 1977

January 5, 1977

There is nothing like working in an emergency room. I do volunteer work at Mass General Hospital. Once a week I spend the afternoon there and I love it. It's not that I love all the blood and gore I see, eyes hanging out, heart attacks, knife gashes all across chests and all across faces. But there is something real about an emergency room that I don't find elsewhere. The people that come in here are in as real a state as can be. They have no barriers up, no defenses. They aren't being false in any way since they aren't caring about their pride when their life is on the line. Why is it that when people are facing death, they are most alive?

February 27, 1977

Poems can no longer be written.

It has been decreed.

Only on the back of the first draft of a lab report

that will no longer be needed

to hand in.

Nonsense must be spared.

Fantasies sacrificed.

For we all know that the Day of Judgment

will be upon us.

It's coming faster. Each morning it gets closer

and closer and closer. So we must hurry to keep

up with the pace that always seems

to run ahead of us.

Hurrying to keep up with the exam

or the exam or

The Exam.

In fact, it has been planned out well.

This way there isn't any space or time

to feel some sunshine,

remember warmth,

and get confused.

April 25, 1977

I had heard through the grapevine that Lois Bloomberg's psychiatrist had cured her of anorexia. Thank God she moved to another dorm this term, Elliot House, so I haven't had to see her. But today I nearly bumped into her in the Square. It was hard not to. She has ballooned, and she is nearly unrecognizable. Her lovely, delicate features are all grotesquely stretched out now. In just a matter of months this happened. I wanted to shriek. She was coming out of Brigham's ice cream parlor, absorbed in an ice-cream cone when I saw her and she looked oblivious to everything else. Thank God she didn't see me. I turned around and walked in the other direction as fast as I could. I didn't look back at all. I was so scared her thick fingers would somehow reach out and grab me. *That's* what's considered "cured!"

May 5, 1977

Today was a turning point. That sounds so stupid. You can't see that you're at a turning point, while you're turning. But *I* can see it this very minute. I can really see it. Everything that happened doesn't seem real. But it was.

Michael has been doing a lot of "power-seeking" lately. And he's made friends in high places. So, somehow I got invited with him to one of the most exclusive garden parties at Harvard given by the Porcelain Club.

I was so scared someone would discover the mistake they had made. What would they do if they found out there was someone *Jewish* at the garden party? Would they actually throw me out? I mean, Harvard *is* pretty liberal now. When it comes to the Final Clubs though, you can see that at the center things really haven't changed that much. But then I figured, why would anyone suspect me, once I was already there? My name isn't especially Jewish. And I don't really look Jewish anymore. My nose is nice, and I'm tan and thin now. All those years of dieting *have* been worth it. What a culmination! I could be thin and rich-looking like every other woman who would be there.

When I got to the party, all I kept thinking was, "This is *it*. I have made it." I thought I had made it to the top before, but, wow, way up here you can *really* get dizzy. I was at the Garden Party people don't even *dream* of attending. Me! A one-time chubby, frizzy-haired, middle-class Jewish girl from Queens. Me! Brushing my bony shoulder past the sons and daughters of the most powerful people in the world. It was such a joy to revel in. Standing there, classically poised in my white halter-style sundress, *I FIT IN!* And I even had the look down of not looking excited about it right, too.

So I figured I'd just stroll on over and talk with my casual acquaintances, Caroline Kennedy and her cousin, Robert F., Jr. Then I figured after that, I'd kind of glide over there by the dainty tea sandwiches and chat for a while with a Rockefeller and a Moynihan, the U.N. Ambassador's daughter. But I couldn't move. I was afraid to breathe. The kind of people that come to these things sure don't do deep-breathing exercises to try and relax. All their breathing is done casually. I don't even think they smell when they perspire. And I knew much better than to blink. If I closed my eyes for just one extra moment, the whole scene would disappear. *I mean, how could it be real?* I kept asking myself. It looked straight out of some fantasy or *The Great Gatsby.* I just stood there thinking, *How did I get to be here on this hedge-enclosed, perfectly-trimmed lawn, among these people?* And then the answer came. *By running away...*

I started running away years back, didn't I? The deepest discussions at a Passover *Seder* in our house were about how fluffy the matzo balls were, between huge mouthfuls. I slammed the door shut on all the mediocrity. Their lower-middle-class tentacles were trying to suck me in, too, but I wouldn't let them. I was different. I was so un-Jewish and airy. I was the kind of person who loved to run through meadows and forests and across beaches in the wind, barefoot, with hair flowing, and in my beautiful faded jeans. And I was going to get out of their clutches and become something great. Something non-Jewish, rich, beautiful, famous, and slender.

But there I was, finally at the Garden Party that had

surpassed my dreams. With no place higher up I could even imagine. And all I was doing was standing there, feeling relieved that nobody had noticed me looking any different from them.

So I began moving…slowly, from one group of people to another. I was dying to find out what the very rich and beautiful said to each other. It felt like my ears were going to jump off the sides of my head, I was so anxious to hear.

And after a while, I found out what they say to each other. It slowly began to dawn on me that *everybody* there was doing the same thing I was doing. Everyone looked like they were dying to hear words of significance. Eyes were darting about, straying far from the people talking to them. Mostly, there was a lot of light laughter.

I did find one group of people talking animatedly. But then I couldn't get over it. They were just discussing a *Newsweek* article, like *anybody* could! I think I liked most listening to the sound of the ice cubes clinking in glasses. It seemed so appropriate. It was like I was inside a big glass there with lots of other human ice cubes, clinking.

And every moment there felt frozen, too. The whole thing seemed too much like a cliché' to be real. But then I guess that's how the clichés came about—describing the way things actually are. There, on the top of the mountain of fame and fortune, was *nothing*. It was so hard to accept. Yet I felt as if, *right then*, the entire scene was being impressed into the deepest recesses of my mind, melting in there. *Aunt Trudy, come and sing the praises of fluffy matzo balls! It would be thrilling compared to this! Everybody at this elite party is bored, through and through.* And it was *exhausting*, having to look expressionless for so long.

Then all of a sudden, I felt like a gigantic cloud had lifted. That's really funny because just as I was starting to think about how really wonderful it was that the garden party was a great big bore, more and more dark, storm clouds were beginning to fill up the sunny sky. It had turned out that there honestly was nothing special about the big shots in the world. I was given the chance to see that they also have nostrils close up, but with no different life breath inside. And just a half-hour before, I would have sold my soul to be one of them.

So I started thinking, what *is* left to strive for, then? If there was nothing up there on the peak of *this* mountain, is there nothing at all above it? *Right then*—I am not kidding, it almost sounds too unreal to put in a *movie*, but *just at that moment*—the clouds broke! A terrific thunderstorm came pouring down on all the white halter dresses and tanned, bony shoulders. It came down on all the white tablecloths and white table umbrellas. It came down on all the perfectly spread tea sandwiches and the whole shebang instantly turned into a sloshy mess. All the guests frantically ran off the manicured lawn to find shelter so that their naturally-styled hair wouldn't get ruined. The privileged garden party collapsed before my eyes instantaneously.

I went skipping home, alone, all the way back to the Radcliffe dorms. I didn't even want to find out where Michael was. It must have been years since I had gone skipping through the streets. But on this gray, transformed rainy afternoon, Cambridge was glistening for me. I skipped back to my dorm, singing and splashing in puddles and thinking. There *is* something more. Something above all that. Something greater. My eyes had been wide open. The next generation's potentially most powerful had been there at The Garden Party. And they couldn't stop the rain from falling down.

June 26, 1977

When my parents came up to Boston for my Harvard graduation, they were shocked at what I looked like. Why does my mother hate it so much that I'm thin? I think I'm finally starting to look really good. I mean, of course I'd still like to lose a little weight, but aside from that I think I really look fine now. What's her problem?

July 5, 1977

I was selected to work this summer in the New York City Mayor's Management Internship Program. Sounds real prestigious, right? What a joke! I work for this agency and all I do is alphabetize the clients' names in the filing cabinet, from eight to five every day. There are two good things about the job, though: the pay is nice and also I don't have to use my brain at all, which is really great because I'm still dieting. Every day I eat just about the same thing. I've got it all planned out. For breakfast I have a piece of fruit, at lunch-break I eat a yogurt, half a cantaloupe with bran sprinkled on top, and for dinner I usually have half a head of lettuce and two pieces of cheese. But sometimes when I can't help myself, I go off my diet at dinner a little, and have a bagel or two, but I feel so horrible afterwards. Then after dinner, I go to exercise at Elaine Powers Figure Salon. It's hard to get out of bed in the mornings, but once I get started I really have a lot of energy the rest of the day. I even feel like a kid again; light and airy and lots of pep. I love being thin like this.

July 14, 1977

Every woman I see I'm thinking, *Is that woman thinner*

than me? Is that one? or, *She's too heavy, she must be miserable.* And *I'm* not? I'm even more miserable than the heavy women because I can't stop thinking like this. But at least I'm thin. So I don't *look* miserable.

July 17, 1977

There is another college student also doing the stupid alphabetizing with me. Her name is Mindy Rosen, and she is at Cornell, entering her senior year in September. And it's the most incredible thing. She is also obsessed with dieting, just like me. We talk all day while we're alphabetizing and that's practically all we talk about. We tell each other exactly what we ate the previous day, we both know exactly how many calories are in everything, and now I just realized that we are in this daily competition with each other. We're competing in who can eat less each day. And neither of us is admitting that we're doing this whole sick thing.

August 1, 1977

Dear Leah,

Can you believe that we haven't spoken with each other since graduation day? Sometimes it's hard to believe that our years at Harvard are over already. That was it. Now we're supposed to live our lives. Tonight I am wishing so much that I could just go upstairs to your old room in the dorm and we could hang out, talking for hours like we used to.

I just finished watching this incredibly beautiful TV movie about dying. It was about a young Swedish woman dying of cancer. I just looked in the newspaper to find out what the name of the movie was, and it was called *Love your Life* which may sound corny, but that is exactly what I have been thinking about these last few weeks. There are so many, many thoughts I have which I have not shared with anyone yet. The only place I have expressed them partially is in the journal I keep. I hope so much that I will have the courage now to write all that I want to write to you.

I am now for the first time ready and willing and *anxious* to give up my obsession. I was never willing to give it up before. I want to dwell as little as possible now in the Land of Obsessive Concern About Dieting, Eating Disorders, and Weight. I have been living in that Land, and I have been very unhappy there.

During the past years, I have become increasingly concerned about my weight. I have never been anorexic or obese, but I've lived in a constant alternating fear that I was going to become either one or the other. Although I became gradually more aware of my obsession, I was afraid to stop being obsessed. There was always this lurking terror in the back of my mind that if I ever stopped being super concerned and "on guard" and let the reins relax for too long, I would slide into obesity.

I always wanted to keep it as "My Secret Problem." Why am I willing to bring it out into the open now? Well, there are quite a few reasons, and I'm not sure which is the strongest.

One reason is that I really have been losing a lot of weight (I weigh ninety pounds now). I am starting to be afraid that I am becoming anorexic, and I don't at all want that. I like the way I look and don't want to be thinner, but I have been and still am (but now I am trying to work on it) terrified of becoming fat.

A second reason I'm starting to change about this issue is

that I feel my obsession started years ago when a guy, Stan, that I first really liked as a boyfriend (but who became my closest friend instead) fell for this girl who was so very skinny. I felt then like a completely unattractive, undesirable, and unfeminine blob. And there were a whole unbearable ton of socials at camp where nobody ever once asked the blob to dance either. I guess those feelings never really went away; it hurt so very much. It was like that whole painful time ingrained in me that to be considered attractive, in fact to be considered at all, one has to be thin. And it became so super-important to me deep inside. I buried these feelings even from myself because they were much too painful to look at them. My ideas about attractiveness were confirmed when, after returning from a summer vacation fifteen pounds slimmer, Stan suddenly "fell in love" with me.

Well, anyway, I met that same girl (Debby) that Stan had been attracted to years ago, in a department store last week. It was a complete shock. She was quite a bit heavier than me. What a jolt I got from that. And suddenly I felt so much better about everything.

I don't even understand why seeing her recently made me feel the way it did, but it was like, there we were, standing face-to-face together in this store, and I had finally achieved that great feat of being thinner than this Other Woman, and I was thrown smack up against the Truth. *Big deal*! Look, being thin actually, unbelievable as it may seem, is *not* the most important thing in the world! My thoughts were, *You've gotten where you wanted to be. So what if you relax for now? If you get afraid, you can always come back. Now you know that you can do it, if you want to.* There was a moment when everything was clear. The obsessive dieting seemed so incredibly foolish. And somehow I don't think this very personal set of events leading up to my obsession is as peculiar as it may appear. I have a feeling similar personal experiences may help to trigger weight obsessions in many other women.

Michael is the only person who knows how thoroughly obsessed I am. I would always go to him after I would have an eating binge at school, completely hysterical and hating myself so much. Well, what happened was, the day before I met that girl, Debby, in the department store, I had eaten like crazy and called up Michael in Washington, D.C., completely hysterical. Maybe what made it even worse was that there he was in D.C., working in a soup kitchen. He's trying to give food to poor people that don't have enough to eat and there I was, crying to him like a spoiled baby because I had gorged myself with food that day. He sounded like he was fed up with listening to me rant about this subject, and said I should go talk to a counselor. And my parents want me to go to a counselor now, too. I had wanted to be so nice with Michael on the phone since it was the first time we had talked since he had left for D.C., and here I'd finally gotten the chance to talk to him, and what did I do? Spent the whole time being hysterical with him about "My Secret Problem."

When I hung up the phone, I felt a very strong sense of disgust toward myself. I had allowed this obsession to take such control over me that there was no more room for any good feelings in our relationship. It seemed like all I wanted him for now was to be my own personal Confession Box.

O.K., here comes another reason for wanting to finally get rid of this sickness, which is devouring me. This summer I am working in an office with a woman who has become the closest thing I have to a friend here right now. And she, I came to learn, is even more entrenched within this horrible Land than I am. In many ways, it is like having a mirror held up to me. I was able to come to see my own obsession in an outside-looking-in sort of way.

And last, but not least, in just over two weeks, I will be going to medical school. Being obsessed with gaining weight has drained the energy from my creativity, my enthusiasm for living, and from my love of other people. I just suddenly saw it so clearly. If I gain weight, *big deal*, there is so, *so* much more. As obvious as that may sound, it is a constant struggle (but maybe now it will be a slightly easier one) for me to be comfortable with that more relaxed view.

They sent me my medical school syllabus. They sent me, believe it or not, exactly what I will be studying for every single weekday from 8 to 5 for the entire year next year, right down to each specific hour! There is so much to learn in order to help others, so much to learn in order to become a wonderful therapist, which I really want to be. My love and my energy are my most important tools. I need them back. I can't sacrifice them just to be excessively vain about my looks.

I was reading through things I wrote when I was younger and seeing how the warmth and energy had gotten lost along the way. And it *was* in me once, so it must still be there if I try to get to it.

Oh Leah, it is going to always be an uphill struggle to rearrange priorities. They have been set in this distorted fashion for several years. It will not be at all easy to stop this internal chatter that goes on in my brain. To shift it from constantly talking about how not to gain weight to talking about so many other wonderful things that there are to think about in life. It will also not be at all easy to stop fearing that this change in my thinking, this "relaxing of the reins," will lead to me getting fat. But oh God, I am willing to try. It's funny, functioning at half capacity for so long, I *almost* totally forgot what functioning at a much fuller capacity was like. Imagine having all of my energy available for whatever activity I am involved with at the moment!

Women are instructed non-stop through the media that the way they look physically is of dire importance. Women are repeatedly taught that they will not know happiness unless they are attractive to the opposite sex through their appearance. So women continually make themselves more and more miserable in an attempt to attain that mirage of happiness. I want other women to know that I am a woman who considers herself a feminist. And feminists too— probably *many* of them—still believe deep inside so many of The Great Big Lies we have been told.

It really is a new thing for me to see that being physically attractive does not equal happiness. I want to stop spending so much of my time fighting, and once again become friends with food. I don't want to be in a constant battle against it. I just want to think of it as one of the things that helps to sustain life.

Although I'm just beginning to give up my overriding concern with dieting and weight control, it already feels like an enormous "weight" is going to be lifted off of me. I would like, in the future, to be able to help other women lift similar kinds of "weights" off of themselves. But I am not at all ready for that.

Leah, I hope that somehow all this may be helpful to hear. We never really talked about the subject directly, but I know that you too are concerned a lot with dieting. I know this letter has been totally about me, and you are probably going through all kind of things since graduation. I want very much to hear about how things are going for you this summer, but I just really wanted to pour this out right now.

I really hope you will send me your reaction as soon as it is possible. Otherwise, I will feel like I'm dangling off a ledge.

Love,

Joanne

P.S. I'm also getting tired of wearing black. How about you?

August 21, 1977

Well here I am at South Carolina Medical College. It is very strange here. Like an entirely different world. Everybody has a Southern accent and a can of beer in one hand. Everyone is always "partying." I didn't picture med school like this. The dorm I'm in is only for women, and practically all the women are nursing students. I feel very alone here...and frightened.

August 30, 1977

I wanted to come down to the South to get further away from my background, but never knew what my background was before this. I'm so different than the people here. Everyone just wants to fool around and escape thinking. This is nothing like Harvard was. And I have a feeling this is how most people like to live. But why do I feel that what makes me different than all these people is that I'm Jewish? Some people here had never met a Jew before. One classmate from a small farm around here really thought that Jews had horns. Most of my classmates are Southern Baptists. I'm not used to the loud, slap-happy, crass way the guys talk. Maybe I'm just homesick.

September 11, 1977

I never went to a dance at Harvard. I didn't even know people that went. But here, they have one almost every Friday night. And everyone goes. This guy, Jack, a second-year medical student, picked me up at the dance Friday night. We left the dance and went out to a string of bars. How can I be acting like this?

September 27, 1977

Jack is a lot of fun, but he must be an alcoholic. Or is he just like any regular person here? He takes me out to different discos and bars nearly every night. Each one I can't believe exists. In a way, it reminds me here of what I heard the 1950's were like. Don't they know down here in the South that times have changed? I'm beginning to wonder myself. I don't think they know that feminism exists here. Even the instructors make jokes about women throughout their lectures. And everyone laughs. Nobody would have ever *dared* to make one tiny wisecrack about women at Harvard.

All these bars and discos seem scarily surreal. Like they were put here as backdrops, just for me to see. Jack drinks all the time. I never drank as much in my whole life as I do now in just one night. How come I'm having fun acting this stupid way? Following him around to all these cheap places. I just never knew this kind of low life really existed before, and it's like a horror show I'm dying to see.

Nobody studies here. But I'm not doing too well on the quizzes they've given so far. I can't even tell a nerve from an artery! Everyone else seems to be doing fine. I can't understand it. Everyone thinks because I went to Harvard, this all must be a breeze for me. I can't study anymore. What's happened to my brain?

September 29, 1977

Now I talk in a whisper with a Southern accent! Even though I'm the one from the big city, I *am* the one who's really naive.

October 3, 1977

Jack is finished with me. When I expressed some very tentative, open feelings to him, his eyes turned icy and he said to me with such hatred, "Don't try to put any strings on me." After that, he wanted to drive me away from his life, as fast as he could. When he dumped me out of his car, outside my dorm, I knew my warmth, my needs, my openness had turned him off and he would never call me again. I just stood there in the parking lot late last night, feeling like I really had no place to go and no one to go to. I just stood there, after getting out of his car, choking on pain that was stuffed down, way too deep to come out.

But why did I feel, standing out there in the parking lot, as if the word "Jewess" was impressed right on top of me in bold, black letters? That's all I was feeling, *shameful* and *Jewish*, more starkly than ever, ever.

October 8, 1977

I want to leave medical school but there is nothing else I want to do. I can't stand all the loneliness. Really, I just want to get married and have a family. If I say it, people will think I am kidding around.

Nobody here seems to have morals. I hate the horrible scene with men, and trying to meet someone. I'm so sick of it.

Isn't there anyone out there for me, someone with a good heart, someone *genuinely* loving. Guess it's too much to ask for. When I pass Jack in the halls after classes, he looks through me as if I do not really exist.

November 2, 1977

At the school's Halloween Masquerade Party, there were all these people with horrible masks. The whole campus was there. We were all stoned, all the masks seemed real, and it was scary down through my blood vessels because I was sure that what I saw that night was real and everyone really did want to get me. Get me and stuff more and more garbage down my throat like they've been doing. So I'd stop thinking and feeling and get laid back like them. I felt like they'd like to stuff up my insides with garbage and let me choke. I still can't shake off the feeling completely.

All-night diners and bars are really out there; full of all these regular kind of people I've never met before in my life. Like The Donna Reed Show and Ozzie and Harriet. So TV was real? Or I was real? Which one is real?

Now I *know* there is more to this world than what we just normally see before us. There are a million different layers to life. I always couldn't give up thinking there is more to life than what there appears to be. But now I've *seen* it. Now I have my own proof. There are many levels to reality. Many dimensions that we don't see in this narrow existence we're normally living.

November 23, 1977

I've been gaining a lot of weight. I sure don't fit into the size three clothes I brought with me. I went out and bought some new things. I never used to eat candy bars. Now when I find a machine and no one is around, I buy six at once. I'm on the meal-plan, but I miss most of the meals in the cafeteria, so I won't eat too much, and then I go to the basement of the dorm and buy twelve candy bars (I make two trips).

I'm too nervous to sit down and study. My head is already saturated with facts about fats. I have to keep track of the exact number of calories in every food I might have to come in contact with. How could I have any room left to memorize the names of all those nerves and veins and arteries!

December 20, 1977

I'm so relieved that Anatomy is over with. All those big, bloated bodies we dissected. Some people were jumping rope with one cadaver's large intestine on the last day of Anatomy in celebration. My cadaver was a middle-aged, obese woman. I'll never forget all the gloppy, greasy yellow fat in her dissected body. Is that all a big body is, a pile of gloppy fat?

Chapter Eight: January 19, 1978—June 7, 1978

January 19, 1978

Michael called me from Boston today for my birthday. I wanted to sound cool and detached, but I couldn't stop crying the minute I heard his voice. It was awful trying to talk to him out there on the dorm's public phone. All the giggly nursing students on my floor were listening, and I had to scream into the phone for him to hear me.

Why did Michael and I drift apart? I guess just because we are living in different places now, meeting different people. We're both seeing others now, and pretending to each other that we're happy. After we hung up, I went back to my room and re-read things Michael had written to me like, "Through you, Joanne, I could come close to God" and "I can't live without your warmth, your delightedness." I guess he is managing. And there is no warmth or delightedness left in me anyway.

February 16, 1978

Bill is my boyfriend now. He's in my med school class, and he's a lot of fun. He's got such a great cynical sense of humor. I think my parents would like him, but I couldn't possibly work up the nerve to tell them about him, mainly because his last name is McDonald.

March 14, 1978

There was a poster up about a Bagels and Lox Sunday Morning Brunch on the University campus. So I figured, as always, I should give it one more try. It was horrible, *horrible*. Not one word about Judaism. All these real squares show up to these kind of things. I left when no one was looking. Why don't I just give up? I hate myself for still hoping there might *really* be someone or something there for me. But I just saw an ad in the paper for a Jewish Singles Party next Saturday night. O.K., I'll try again. You never know.

March 20, 1978

Now I know. I took three busses to get to the Jewish Singles Party, then I was totally embarrassed to even be there. And I was so desperate to leave, I had this guy who was super drunk, drive me back to the dorm. How can I let drunkards drive me home? Because, who cares? My stomach was sick from too much food, but really from despair. This Jewish guy I was with wasn't for me either, I'm so, so afraid there will never be anyone for me.

March 22, 1978

I can't bear to face myself. Why am I doing this? Before every exam I'm getting extremely nervous now. I don't want to take any more exams. I'm so sick of all these tests.

I walk downtown into a department store and buy a bag of white chocolates with nuts at the candy counter. Then after something sweet, I want something heavy and greasy or something warm and smothery. I go to a fast-food place and get a greasy hamburger and a large bag of French fries.

After that, to another store for a milk shake, then something non-sweet again like a tuna fish sandwich in a coffee shop, and then two doughnuts from a bakery "to go" and a diet soda (every calorie counts). The whole time I'm shaking terribly, more and more, so terrified someone will notice I'm the same person that was eating in a place a few stores down. Always hiding as I eat. Finally, finally I'm out of money, but I'm still starving…and shaking so much. My stomach is bursting, but I just don't feel full. I always want more.

March 28, 1978

I don't just gorge myself before I have to take an exam. I have to eat now before I can start anything new, like sitting down to study, or walking into the bank, or even making certain phone-calls. And I always tell myself I just need this one scrumptious-looking cookie—it can't hurt—and then I'll surely be alright; after I eat it, *everything* will be alright. But then a few minutes later, after I've scraped out every last crumb from the corners of the wax paper lining in the box and the entire box of cookies is empty, I feel empty, too. And I have to find something else to eat very, very quickly. I get frantic if I can't get my hands on something to eat right away. It's scary until I get the next thing.

It's so great while I'm in the middle of munching on a 'family size' bag of potato chips, each delightful candy bar, sandwiches with lots of extra creamy mayonnaise dripping over the sides, a jar of Super Crunchy peanut butter (down to the last yummy lick!), a package of Gouda cheese, a package of American cheese, and then from a snack machine, a cherry Pop Tart pie or two or three (for dessert). But when each one gets finished, I'm left just facing miserable me again. And I can't stop. I continually need more to escape from myself.

But no matter how much I put in, it is never enough. I always think it will be.

How do normal people know when to stop eating? Do other people really eat something like a sandwich and feel like it's all they need; that it's *enough*; that they're *completely satisfied*? How can that be? As I'm eating something, I'm sure that's absolutely the only thing I want. I really think the joy I have while I'm munching happily away will never end. I'm hoping each luscious bite will last a lifetime, and I won't have to face myself when it's all through. Why can't those magic moments while I'm eating a candy bar and the world seems so sweet just go on and on? Why are candy bars all made too short?

At some point during the binges, I'm no longer devouring everything because I feel like I need the food. No, I switch to eating more food because I hate myself so much for having eaten so much. I'm so angry that I stuff more and more food into my face. I stop craving the food and start hating it for hurting me. I eat slower and slower because it is more and more difficult to chew it all up. Even a chocolate cookie becomes incredibly nauseating and almost impossible to eat, but I keep pushing more and more into my mouth.

Really it's not just when I'm nervous that I need to eat. Sometimes plans get changed and I'm a little disappointed, so I eat because I guess I feel I deserve something, *some* comfort. And if something unexpectedly nice happens, I have to eat desperately right away also because I don't know what else to do with the happiness. It sort of terrifies me.

I think I need something else in me because I can't face the world alone just as I am, running on empty. I think I just figured out what I'm so afraid of: life.

March 30, 1978

Today was a good day. I had an orange for breakfast. I peeled it very, very slowly, ate each section of orange singularly, and then caught each drop of juice that fell, savoring it. I tried to make it last as long as possible. I didn't eat lunch at all, then only four giant carrots for dinner.

Tomorrow I will eat the same thing. I can do it. I just have to walk very quickly past the school cafeteria on my way to classes and also on the way coming home; that's the biggest danger zone. I just have to force my legs to move past it, keep my head turned away from it, and my eyes looking at something straight ahead. If I can do that, I'll really feel in control. But lunchtime is the hardest. Sometimes I stay in a medical school bathroom until it's over. I just lock myself into a toilet stall until it's all over and I don't have to watch everyone else eating the brown bag lunches that I want to grab out of their hands. Dinner isn't hard to miss. I just go to sleep instead. Once I fall asleep I'm not hungry again until the next morning.

April 1, 1978

Today, when I was out bingeing on food downtown, a scary-looking guy started following me. He was lurking there behind me, *every* place I went. I ran into a big department store and kept running down the aisles and finally lost him there. My heart was racing so fast. I can't go back to all those stores anymore.

April 8, 1978

After classes are over, I wait around and pretend to study, then I go through the garbage pails. I start on one floor and then I go searching through all the garbage pails in the building. People throw out such great food! Why should all this perfectly good food go to waste? I like best all the partially-eaten sandwiches. There are so many different kinds people get. This way I get to try things I'd never buy on my own. Like ham and cheese and mustard. That's a real find! Waste not, want not. I've got it down to an art now. I wait around 'till no students can be seen. I can't wait too long, though, because the janitor comes and dumps all the garbage pails. Sometimes on really lucky days, doctors have little receptions in meeting rooms and they leave over lots of sandwiches and cookies and cake. I eat every last crumb; even if soda is poured all over them and everything. I just spit out the shreds of paper napkin that get mashed into the food. The more soggy and squashed it is in the garbage pail, the better I feel about eating it all up.

April 20, 1978

Sometimes there isn't enough in the garbage pails on all the floors of the medical school building. I can't go back to the cafeteria by the dorm to eat where everyone will watch me and I'm embarrassed to keep taking more and more portions, so I take things out of the refrigerators here, in the lounges where the residents and interns go for breaks and store their food. If I see that the food has been in the fridge for a few days, no one probably wants it anyway.

April 23, 1978

People have started putting up nasty notes on the fridge to whoever is stealing the food, but I can't stop myself now. I know when no one is around and I take whatever is in there.

I really think I don't have any morals left…about anything. There's no black and white. The whole world is a drab gray. It doesn't matter what I do.

April 25, 1978

In our dorm, there is a fridge, too. I had eaten only a few carrots for the past two days, and last night when I went to the dorm fridge to take out more of my carrots, there was a whole big salami in there, so I ate it. Today my friend Kathy comes and tells me how disgusting it is that someone in our dorm is stealing food. Here she had a brand new salami and someone took it! She said how if someone had wanted some and asked her, she would have been happy to give it. But how low can a person be to steal other people's food! I just sat there agreeing with her and saying, "Ugh! How could anyone do a disgusting thing like that?"

April 26, 1978

I think one of the janitors knows what I'm doing. He almost caught me today.

April 28, 1978

Bill told me I get too upset about gaining weight. He said I really should go to a therapist here who counsels medical school students, but I'm scared it will go on my record. God, if he only knew the whole story. But I think I am going to have to go. I don't want to go on like this.

May 4, 1978

I told the therapist, Dr. Sands, everything, *everything*! At first I thought I'd just tell him a little, but then everything started to spill out. I had to get it all out. I feel better, in a way, not to have it all inside me, alone, anymore. I felt like I was going crazy. He said he is referring me to another therapist who deals with my kind of problem.

May 12, 1978

Dr. Wang was nice, but he doesn't seem to think I'm so crazy. I was hoping he'd tell me they are going to give me a break from school. I'm just so tired of thinking. I want to rest and not think anymore. I need a good, deep rest. What is there to live for?

May 15, 1978

Last night, I was in another sleazy bar on The Strip, and there was a bar brawl between two loud drunks. Some huge guys fell over during the fight, down *onto* me, and I got knocked off my stool and hit the floor. It smelled of spilled liquor and urine and vomit down there. Someone spit their stinking saliva on me and I wanted to scream, "I am not like you!" But who would have cared? Who would have believed me?

When I could, I made it out the door to the street, and I crouched there on the sidewalk, by the gutter. And something half-forgotten came back then—those dreams I had years back—they were about *these* scary streets. They were about this gutter. From the pit of my stomach, I could hear one tiny voice, crying out of the numbness, "God, *please*, pick me up. Pull me up from this gutter."

May 26, 1978

At my second session with Dr. Wang, I told him that the very last-minute plans had *actually* come through, and I will be going to Israel for the summer. I still can't get over his reaction. He said that I am not nuts like I think I am; that when I go to Israel this summer I will find what I have been looking for. He said my Jewish soul is searching, and when I find what I'm looking for, only then will I be fulfilled. Maybe *he's* the one that's nuts. He *really* believes I'm going to find something there. That's not the kind of thing therapists are supposed to say! And a Japanese one yet, saying this to me! But somehow he made me so happy.

June 2, 1978

I'm home now for a week before I go to Israel. This whole trip was my mother's doing. I know why she arranged the whole thing. She wants me to meet "a nice Jewish guy" (translation: boring). So she got me this volunteer job at Hadassah Hospital for six weeks. I asked to be placed on the oncology ward. I want to be with the patients who are dying.

We just found out that a friend of my mother's committed suicide. She called my Mom for advice two days ago. My Mom had asked *my* advice. What should she say to her friend who has this terrible life? She's divorced and her daughters are both addicts that literally steal from her every penny she makes. I told my mom, if I was that woman, I'd kill myself. Today we found out that she did.

Some great psychiatrist I'd make.

June 4, 1978

My Mom told me the one thing she *doesn't* want me to do when I go to Israel is contact Mark Weiss, an old friend of mine from the neighborhood. He became a religious fanatic. He is learning in an ultra-Orthodox yeshiva in Israel.

So *of course*, right away I called up his mother the first chance I had, got his address, and wrote him a letter. I told him when I am coming to Israel and that I'll be staying at the Hadassah Hospital dorms. I wrote that I'd love to take some part-time courses about Judaism in the evenings, if he could show me where they are given. I wrote to him that I want to know what the purpose of life is so I can be a good psychiatrist.

June 6, 1978

Dear Joanne,

I didn't want to make our parting at the airport too maudlin, but there are some things I still want to say. I can honestly say that my happiest moments were spent in your company, but we let thoughts about the future intervene into the present and something happened.

Your religion doesn't matter to me. You know that. I wouldn't hold it against you. You are free to grow stronger in your faith with me. I would want to share that with you as well.

I expect to see a much stronger person in August than I left at the airport. I want to see a happy woman instead of a woman-child.

Stay in touch. What you're doing interests me more than anything else in the world right now.

I'm good for you, and I hope you realize it one day.

All my love,

Bill McDonald

June 7, 1978

I looked around my room tonight with such a funny feeling. Is this what people mean when they feel "butterflies" in their stomachs? I'll be leaving on the plane for a six-week visit to Israel in a few hours. Why do I feel like I may not come back?

Chapter Nine: June 10, 1978—June 27, 1978

June 10, 1978

Dear Joanne,

Hi! I hope you are enjoying yourself in Israel. My small hometown hasn't changed a bit in the past year. Even the gossip remains the same.

You ought to have your greatest summer ever. Do whatever seems right for you. Stop being so serious. That's not your style. You were made to be happy, and you will be.

Shalom,

Bill

June 10, 1978

Jerusalem, Israel

"My Neighborhood"

What makes me want to crawl back home?

A map.

Drawn in elementary school

That says

"My Neighborhood."

With all the colored

Cardboard doors and street-lamps.

And all the shopkeepers with

Friendly smiles

Of Elmer's glue.

What makes me want to crawl back home?

The excited voices of

Everyone

Going off to school

In the morning.

And me hearing them all

Because I lived

Across the street from the

Schoolyard.

What makes me want to crawl back home?

Poster paints and dioramas.

Passing notes to

Special friends with special secrets.

Constructing leaf people,

Colorforms,

Playing the "triangle"

In a marching band.

What makes me want to crawl back home?

No matter how I try to put

The Magic into now,

It will not fit.

A box of cookies

As a temporary refuge

Doesn't last long.

Not long enough

To be a kid forever.

June 11, 1978

There isn't much for me to do here at Hadassah Hospital. I have a feeling now that somebody was just being nice to my mother in letting me come. There really is *nothing* for me to do. The patients only speak Hebrew, except for one. That patient, Avi, is a wonderful man with a lovely Israeli wife, Tzippy. He is a poet, an English professor at Bar Ilan University, and he is originally from New York. He is probably about thirty-five, with two little daughters, and he is a living skeleton. He looks almost like an embryo, curled up on the bed in a deformed way, his head so out of proportion in size to his shrunken body. Yet, he always manages to have a smile for me and a friendly greeting when I come into his room.

June 12, 1978

I have never been as alone as I am now, 7,000 miles away from all the people I care about, and that care at all about me. I don't even speak the same language as the people here. They all think I'm strange. I'm spending a lot of time alone in this tiny dorm room they gave me. I guess that's what I'm supposed to be doing this summer…facing myself. That's really all I've got now.

June 13, 1978

I don't want to be alone. Take care of me. I don't want to be alone. Take care of me. Don't just stand there, Mom and Dad. Take care of me. Do something. You did when I was little. Then what? Where did all that wonderful love go? Take care of me. I don't want to grow up. I'm afraid of all the Big Bad Monsters out there. The men on the loose. I don't trust what they're after from me. They don't want the real me.

Remember when I was able to run, run, run down hills and all around? When I had the freedom to be powerful, filled with energy; an attractive energy everyone wanted to be near. A radiant energy. I want it now. I want to feel alive again. It has been so, so long. What happened? I got afraid. I stopped running…and I stopped *running my life! So that's* when I stopped running my life! Writing plays, making up songs, creating things, I used to be so creative when I was a child.

What happened? Why did I get so afraid? I felt like I lost control. There was a whole new set of games to play, with totally unfamiliar rules. And I was a failure at those new games; never picked to dance at any "socials." Year after year, I sat there, so desperately waiting. And what if I am left all alone? And you too, Mommy, would you leave me? *You too? Why?* Just because I was getting too old for you to love me the way you used to? Too old for me to rest and cuddle in your arms? Too old for you to surround me and protect me?

But I'm not too big. I'm still young. I'm still your little girl. Please don't leave me, Mom. I still need you. I am afraid to be on my own. I am afraid to grow up. Let someone else pick the food I will eat. I'll take whatever they leave me. Something left over for me. Some love left over.

I feel in control when I don't eat. I become child-like again. As a child the world seemed so wondrous, but then all the rules changed. I want to be not just safe and warm, but alive in every way. The cold, though, has been so *very* cold.

June 14, 1978

I am going to give up now, for good.

Ten years have gone away from the time when I first began wondering about the purpose of life. And then the question became transformed into: Why do people get up in the morning, go to work, make money, buy food and eat it, in order to live until the next day to do the same thing?

When I was twelve, the basic questions about life began to plague me. And now, ten years later, the answers haven't taken any better form. I haven't gained *any* understanding all this time.

As a child you are supposed to learn about life. And by now, I'm supposed to be living it! But I still don't have any idea what life is all about. Where are the answers I could live with?

Ten years from now, it would be just the same. *So what for?*

June 15, 1978

Yesterday, right after I wrote my last journal entry, I was still sitting alone in the Hadassah Hospital staff cafeteria (mechanically finishing my fourth helping of the dinner being served). When I looked up, and there was my old-friend-turned-religious-fanatic, Mark Weiss, coming toward me with a big smile on his face. I was so thrilled to see him, I jumped up to give him a big hug! But he practically jumped away, laughing that good old laugh of his. He said religious men don't touch women they aren't married to. I couldn't get over it. But anyway, then he sat down and was very nice and friendly. He gave me a book to read, *A Tzaddik in Our Time*. And tomorrow night, I'm going to meet him. He is going to take me to a class on Judaism like I had written him about. I'm so excited! You never know from minute to minute in life.

June 16, 1978

Oh, it was so, so wonderful. Mark took me to a class. He stayed outside the building it was in because the class was only for women. There were about thirty women there. It had already started when I got there, so I sat in the back. A Hasidic-looking rabbi with a long, gray beard and black suit was talking. I ate up every word. And the women asked such intelligent questions. I loved it. It sounds so silly, but do you know what I felt as I was sitting there listening, walking to the bus afterwards, on the whole, long bus ride, and walking back here to my room at Hadassah? I felt the deepest joy. I want to cry forever and scream up to the stars, "Yes, *Yes, YES!*"

June 17, 1978

I hung out at Hadassah this morning, visiting with Tzippy and her husband and having coffee with the chief resident in oncology, Rafi.

On the cover of the book Mark Weiss gave me, there is a picture of the man about whom the book is written. His name is Rabbi Aryeh Levin and he lived here in Jerusalem. He looks like all the religious Jews I see here in the streets; he could be any of them, and I'd never know it. What's great about him, I'd never guess just by looking at him. I'd never guess he was great. But he was. His actions were filled with goodness.

He was devoted to helping the ones that most people don't want to get close to: poverty-stricken people, convicted criminals, lepers. He loved all people. He didn't feel superior to anyone. He took care of forgotten people; sought them out. Rabbi Aryeh Levin was a simple man, but with deep understanding. He lived in a little hole-in-the-wall apartment, but his home was one of true greatness.

You grow up and find out Santa Claus isn't real. But then, when you grow up even more, you find out Santa Claus *can* be real. Rabbi Aryeh Levin was a living example of everything he taught, right down through the smallest, seemingly mundane daily details. A person that truly wasn't a hypocrite! A *tzaddik* is a genuinely good human being. There are still good people in the world.

June 21, 1978

Rafi, the chief resident, asked me to spend the weekend with him in Tel Aviv. It sounds exciting. I think the change will be good for me. I need to get away from this religious stuff a little.

June 23, 1978

Tel Aviv was like "The Strip" in South Carolina, only a pathetic imitation of it. And these were *all Jews*! Nightclubs, all-night discos—we did the whole scene. The streets there were *jammed* with people in their teens and twenties, roaming around all night long Friday night. Everyone looked empty. We were all lost Jews, not knowing what to do but roam. And I hated being with that guy!

June 24, 1978

I went looking for Aish HaTorah yeshiva today, the place where Mark studies. Mark told me there would be a class at his yeshiva today on the basics of Judaism for men and women. When I got to the address I'd written down for the school, I stopped dead in my tracks. Staring me in the face was a poster, taped on the entrance, with a huge blown-up photo of, of all things, a delicious looking bagel, stuffed with cream cheese and lox. And the caption below it read, "Is *this* the culmination of our 3,000-year-old heritage?" I then knew I had found the right place, before I even opened the door.

A big, jovial white-bearded man with a black suit and black hat, Rabbi Noach Weinberg, was giving a class in a long, mostly empty room. I liked that hearty, chuckling rabbi right away.

He was asking a question to his small audience, "Are you eating to live or living to eat?" His words went piercing through me. That was no simple question for me to answer. *He better not call on me for the answer,* I was thinking. *He's got no idea what kind of nut he's got sitting in on his class.*

But then a guy from the back row called out the expected answer, "I'm eating to live!" I was breathing again, and hoping the rabbi would now get off the uncomfortable subject of eating.

"O.K. then, my friend," said Rabbi Weinberg, "So what *are* you living for? Hold on there, Mike, I don't mean to put you on the spot. *Anybody* have an answer?"

It was such a basic question, but not one person there felt ready to give an answer. Rabbi Weinberg broke the slightly too long silence with a chuckle. "People go to school for years to learn how to make a living," he said. "How many years do people spend learning *how to live*?"

This was the class I had envisioned existing somewhere. Maybe I should have come *here* after elementary school! Now I am *finally* at a school that can give me some wisdom about life. My pen couldn't move fast enough to get down all the ideas he presented, but I really worked at it.

"What's the opposite of pleasure?" Rabbi Weinberg asked. And he answered what was probably in all of our minds this time, "Most people answer: pain. Well, in Judaism, we say that the opposite of pleasure is *comfort*, not pain. The soul wants pleasure. The body wants comfort. The soul wants meaning, wisdom, truth, to love. The body wants things like food and luxuries.

"Comfort doesn't last; it's momentary. Soul pleasures are

lasting. Comfort even distracts a person from seeking pleasure. And as you get more and more comfort, like with food for example, if you eat more and more, it stops being enjoyable and actually starts to get even *nauseating*. But with soul pleasures, the enjoyment only increases.

"And what about pain? You can think of pain as an effort. Making an effort is painful, right? Well, if you go over your own lives, you'll see how pleasure only comes through a lot of effort. Effort is the *means* to pleasure. And just like it requires effort to remove the peel from an orange to get at the fruit underneath, it also requires effort to remove the peels, the outer coverings present in life, in order to eat from the ultimate sweetness and extract the lasting pleasures of life. *And wow, what* a juice is concealed inside!

"Our body has desires. It tells us, 'If I don't get that strawberry shortcake, I'm going to die!' And that distracting voice, that encourages you to damage yourself, doesn't openly tell you to eat the whole cake, either. It tells you to eat *just one more piece*. It requires a tremendous amount of effort to ask yourself honestly, 'What do I bow down to—God, prestige, money, or an ice-cream sundae?'"

I was starting to wonder if maybe he *did* know who was in his class. How else could he understand me so deeply? But he was talking to everyone, wasn't he? And I thought this class was supposed to be about the basics of Judaism. *This* is Judaism?

The rabbi was saying, "If you don't know what you're living for, you're a zombie. Why run so fast, if you don't know where you're going?"

Yippee! That's my question!

"This world was created to give us pleasure."

That's *the answer?*

"Our natural state of being is joy. If we don't have that feeling, something is off."

You're telling me! But I thought Orthodox Jews were into being so stiff and serious; all those dark black suits and everything.

"Everyone wants to be good, and everyone thinks he is a good person, even the mass murderer. So what is a good man? Well, some people answer, 'Just do the "natural" thing.' In Judaism, we say a person has to develop himself, sensitize himself to his inner core, and the Torah explains how to go about this."

That inner me—that real *Joanne! Have you been in there waiting all this time?*

"The first time you do something wrong—like stealing, for example—you feel so guilty and anxiety-stricken. Second time, it's not so bad. After the third time, it becomes the right thing to do. A person will sometimes go through any amount of effort to avoid thinking. Thinking is uncomfortable. But the pleasure you get from the wisdom you bring out is great, and it endures. Judaism teaches us how to use and trust our minds to *determine* what is good and which pleasures are real ones."

Boy, am I ready to use my atrophied mind!

"The blessing and the curse of being a Jew is that Jews are thirsty for God, for the absolute. All our Jewish souls were present at Mount Sinai. We all witnessed God's Presence. So we've experienced the ultimate. That's why we Jews are especially never satisfied. We're never satisfied with less than the ultimate.

"Nothing else can satisfy a Jew and give him peace.

Whatever he does, he'll be the best at it, and that's whether it's being a radical or being a criminal, too. Everyone is looking for the ultimate experience. It's all misplaced searching for God. And that's also why Jews make up such a large part of new religious cults like TM, Moonies, Jews for J.C., and so on."

But I had to search elsewhere. The Judaism I'd been handed was only an "ultimate experience" gastronomically. The Jewish food was great, but that's about it.

"Do you believe you have a soul? What is the source of your soul? What do you do with your soul? Do you just ignore it?"

Soul, if you're still there, I don't have to ignore you anymore.

June 25, 1978

I bought a sketch pad and I bring it to all the classes on Judaism I go to. I *never* thought I'd be taking notes in classes that don't give any exams! After classes, I sit outside and sketch. How I used to love to draw as a child. Now I'm drawing again. Colors are coming back to life!

June 26, 1978

They gave us lunch at the women's school. Then I went down to the fridge in the school kitchen, finished off all the leftovers, and got what I could from the garbage. Then I was too nervous to sit for any more classes so I took the bus downtown to Jaffa Road. I had two slices of pizza and then a yummy fruit milkshake they sell near the pizza shop.

Then I bought two more slices of pizza at another pizza place and for "dessert" another fruit shake. Then I had some more pizza…and more shakes. I spent the whole afternoon like this, like a wound-up doll, going back and forth. I'm so confused about changing my life. How can I make the decision that I know I need to make?

Finally, I just escaped into the first movie theater I could find. I sat through two showings of *Ordinary People* with Mary Tyler Moore dubbed in Hebrew, then I went to the lobby of another movie theater and stayed there with chocolate bars and popcorn until it closed down for the night. Then I took the bus back here to the Hadassah dorms. I'm exhausted.

June 27, 1978

Early in the morning

"One More Potato Chip"

One more potato chip.

One more potato chip.

After this, no more will pass between my lips.

I've got to have it.

Can't live without it.

I will take only one more *unnoticeable* bit.

I'd like a thin slice, please.

Another small slice, please.

After this, I *surely* will feel all at ease.

I really need it now.

I deeply need it now.

One more scoop, I'll be contented as a cow.

I'll take one tiny bite.

O.K., just one more bite.

Is there a cure for my insatiable appetite?

Why can't I stop myself from taking more and more and
more and MORE?

Help! I'm trapped inside this body.

I'm a Prisoner of War!

One chocolate chip cookie.

Two chocolate chip cookies.

I can finish up the box, *if* no one is looking.

I've got this hunger.

It's such a hunger.

But when the piece of cake is gone, it's even *stronger*!

While gobbling up the food,

While gobbling up the food,

Why, I am in just the most delightful mood.

But when it's over,

Oh, when it's over,

The emptiness I tried to bury is uncovered.

When will I give in and realize my body is out of control?

It's not my stomach that is hungry.

What's starving is my soul!

Chapter Ten: June 27, 1978—July 30, 1978

June 27, 1978

Before going to bed

Dear Leah,

I took a long walk today with one of the teachers that I feel close to at the women's school. We walked for hours—all afternoon—and I feel like I am beginning to find answers. There really are answers.

The funny thing is that I did almost all the talking when I was with this teacher. She asked me one question that helped me to go ahead and ask myself all the other questions that were waiting in line, until I finally got to the end of my long string of questions. If someone with wisdom like she has had just given me a few hours of their time years back, really listening, would I have been able to come to all this understanding way back then?

She hardly did anything, but it's made all the difference. For the first time, I could listen to my thoughts all the way through, carrying thoughts through to the end. Whoever gets a chance to do that?

I admitted to her what I thought was a deep dark secret; that I couldn't get it out of my head, that all the Bible stories were a bunch of fairy tales.

"O.K.," she said to me, "So you think they are a bunch of fairy tales." That's all. We were both laughing.

Later on, I came out and actually asked her, "What is the purpose of life?" She turned to me and asked, "What do *you* think is the purpose of life?"

Would you believe, for all my wondering about it all these years, I had never really tried to answer the question on my own. How come? Maybe because no one ever asked me to try and come up with an answer.

I hadn't spoken my thoughts out loud like this to someone in such a long time. I've learned to be witty and cynical and sarcastic, even though that's really not my style. And now I am finding people here at the school just come right out and say what's on their heart! And no one tries to shut them up. We're all openly and honestly searching for truth together. I feel like I'm getting back to my natural self.

I told her how some of the Torah ideas I've been hearing in classes are the same psychological principles they are "discovering" now after millions of dollars' worth of research at Harvard. Ideas like cognitive dissonance, "herd" psychology, growth stages. All these things I studied as "new breakthroughs in the field of psychology" have already been in the Torah for thousands of years. And they're just now figuring them out at Harvard!

So anyway, the question about the purpose of life started soaring through my head. And I was thinking as hard as I could, trying to come up with a great answer to the question. But all I could finally think of to say was, "I guess the purpose of life is to be good, whatever that means, but I don't know what it means."

And then she said to me the only thing I think she said today that wasn't really a question or gentle encouragement. She said, "Judaism explains how to be good in a more detailed way than any other religion." I loved her! She didn't sound like the overly friendly Buddhist chanters or even like the sweet Christian Scientists who were dying to convert me. She wasn't saying what I was afraid she'd say; that this was T.H.E. T.R.U.T.H. That's still too scary. She just put it all so flatly. Almost bland. But why still so attractive to me? *Details about how to be good.*

And someone really listened to me today. She wasn't just trying to stuff me up with all her views. She wasn't pushing some religious dogma down my throat. She heard things I had kept inside for years, both the good and the bad. And after I had expressed all my doubts and there were none left deep inside that I hadn't spilled out—they didn't seem so jumbled and confusing or even as powerful as they had felt for all those years, unspoken—I feel like there is room inside me now for some light.

Love,

Me

June 28, 1978

Dear Mom and Dad,

I do not know how in the world to describe the happiness I am feeling. It feels like years and years since I have ever felt so good. For one thing, I know I want to stay here.

Much more to say, but I've taken up the whole postcard.

Love you so!

June 28, 1978

Dear Ms.

It is a pleasure to inform you that you have successfully completed your freshman year of medical studies, and that you are promoted to the second year at the School of Medicine of South Carolina.

Sincerely,

Jesse L. Danfort, M.D.

Dean, School of Medicine

June 29, 1978

Dear Mom and Dad,

This is a very important letter for me. I have been in the process of composing it for years, but it was not ready until now. I want to begin by writing that I love you both dearly. But next, I want to say that, Mom, I am sick of hearing you say (like you did on our tearful phone conversation yesterday) how guilty you feel about letting me go to medical school in South Carolina.

It is ridiculous. Why stop there? Why not feel guilty for everything you have ever done for me my whole life? Everything you have always done to help make me into the person I am today. Can you not see that it is my whole life that has brought me to this point?

If you want to feel guilty, I mean, you're free to, of course, but then what does that reflect about me? If you feel guilty, it means I have failed in some way. That is what you are saying. Do you need to feel guilty that you have created someone who loves beauty, warmth, truth? Do you need to feel guilty that you have helped develop a person that wants to be in a place with other hopeful people, a place in which I really feel I have found the "purpose to living" that has always eluded me until now?

I have found people here who are not full of cynicism. They are full of optimism. Would you really prefer me to stay feeling hopeless? I understand that you are afraid that because of this "idealism," this "naiveté," this "blindness" I have, I'll end up dying an early death out here in the "dangerous" Middle East. You feel that if I did not have this, this very deep spirit growing within me (no matter how I've tried to squelch it at different periods in my life), then I would be able to have the nice, pleasant existence that you would like me to have. Mom, if I did not have this unquenchable spirit, then I would never have the chance to *live*.

Mom, I do not think I will die here in the land of Israel early in my life (hopefully I *will* die here late in my life). But if I do, at least I will have lived. It must come from me, what I truly need to do. And I know I am disappointing you, and it is hurting me. You can never know, but God, somehow (as you would say, Dad,) "that blade of grass is *still* trying to come up through the cement."

I can see your faces so clearly in how disappointed you are in me. But do you understand how disappointed I have been through all these recent years, straight-jacketing myself into the life I felt I wanted to try to have? But it is *not* me. I have felt a lot of pressure to suppress all the things that make me "different." Ignoring my aching, unfulfilled yearning, I could have had such a happy, "secure" life. What can I say?

I feel I have a much greater potential than all that. Like I said when I was president of the National Honor Society in high school, and I gave that speech that made you so proud, I want to develop my *full* potential, not suppress that spark within me that makes me *"me"* more than anything else.

I want to be a good person. I want to be a loving person. I want to be a giver. Please, Mom and Dad, these are not things to be ashamed of when you have a daughter that wants this. Please try not to be ashamed of me. Try to trust in the goodness that you see in me and be glad to see it develop.

Medical school is not for me. It is not truly what I want. It is hard for me to give it up because medical school makes people think well of me. These two words "medical school," whenever I say them, it makes people feel, without knowing anything else about me, that I am a solid, together person; that I am going along a good path. It is very hard for me to give this up. I will have to write to South Carolina and ask for a leave of absence. And what will you tell people? What can I tell you? I understand how ashamed you will feel right now.

All that I can pray for is that in the future, your tears will turn into tears of joy. Please know how deeply thankful I am for all the blessings you have given me. I love you both so much.

June 30, 1978

To Whom It May Concern,

I wish to apply for a leave of absence from South Carolina Medical School. At this point, it is very important for me to learn about the significance of human life. I therefore wish to remain in Israel in order to take courses dealing with this subject. I hope that this plan will meet with your approval.

July 1, 1978

Dear Mom and Dad,

I am thinking of moving out of the Hadassah dorms this week and into the School for the Education of Jewish Women, which is called *Neve Yerushalayim*. I am not sure about this but I figure, if I am considering staying there for at least a year's leave of absence, I should know what it is like to live there. If I don't like it, I can return home July 29, as scheduled.

I know this sounds very weird to say, but for the first time I am beginning to actually believe that there is a Greater Plan. I was not just tossed about haphazardly. I really feel as if God kind of picked me up and brought me here. I hope I don't sound too "spacey" for writing this.

I know I used to be a very happy person. But in recent years, I was increasingly unhappy with myself and increasingly tense. I think the whole eating problem was a manifestation of this inner tension and dissatisfaction. I find a peacefulness when I involve myself in the Jewish way of life, and I want to explore this more fully. If I came back to the States now, I could too easily be swayed from pursuing this path. Jerusalem is the most wonderful place to be to do this kind of learning.

I love you and I do miss you both, too, but I also feel it is very important for my own "mental health" to stay here now.

July 2, 1978

Dear Joanne,

I hope you don't mind receiving a letter that shatters the myth that golden Jerusalem is the center of the universe, but yes, there is a South Carolina. It exists as surely as there's sand in the desert, or a smile on a little girl's lips. As long as the Union has need for a genteel state, as long as planes land here, there lives a South Carolina.

I hope that receiving this letter from South Carolina doesn't disturb your "escape" vacation. If I was in a foreign country around the 4th of July, I would appreciate a letter from any full-blooded American. Hopefully, you will feel the same way. If you don't, tough luck! I had an irresistible urge to write you.

The news I write of can't compete with the excitement of living and working in Israel, but it's all I have to offer you right now. I hope you've had enough experience and fun to match the sparkle that appeared in your eyes, whenever you spoke of Jerusalem before you left. That was something else!

Have a nice 4th of July, belated or otherwise. A family picnic is planned for the day. Afterwards, we'll probably go to the park for fireworks. All we need now is apple pie to complete the picture. Be good, but try to enjoy yourself anyway. I'll see you in August.

Shalom,

Bill McDonald

July 8, 1978

Dear Mom and Dad,

It was wonderful speaking with you yesterday. It is very important to me that you are accepting what I am doing. I feel there are so many indications that what I am doing is deeply right. As you can probably tell from my letters and calls, I don't feel so desperate anymore.

I guess I feel like my spirit isn't suffocating now. I know I'm not exactly doing the "model daughter" routine. What I'm trying to do is follow my heart finally.

Deep, peaceful feelings fill me. It really feels like I'm getting re-in-touch with the beautiful parts of myself with which I had lost contact. I can even see it in the art classes I'm taking here in the evenings. The pictures being drawn have creativity and imagination pouring out of them, as if it had been bottled up for years.

I can't wait to jump up each morning and see a new day. How different it is from all the mornings I would lie in bed wondering what there was to get up for. In South Carolina, I saw many doctors getting drained (and becoming addicted to drugs and alcohol) in the process of giving. I am learning a lot about *chesed* which means giving to others, in Hebrew. I want to develop into a person who can give to others from a source that can never get drained.

The students here—you would love every one of them. They are considerate, intelligent individuals, interested in growing into better human beings. I think if you met them, you'd want them all as your daughters!

The teachers are the best I've ever had; Harvard professors don't even *compare*! They demonstrate brilliance *combined* with warmth, understanding, insight, and a genuine love for people. What more could one want in a teacher? Now that I'm settled in here, I can write more often and we can make less of those super expensive phone-calls.

July 14, 1978

Tzippy called me from Hadassah Hospital here at the school today. Her husband died. I went to visit her. She wanted me to hear tapes of her husband's lectures. We sat on the couch and listened all afternoon, and we were crying together. Then she started screaming. She couldn't stop. She started screaming about all the pain she has gone through, about how unfair life is, about how cruel people are, and then she began attacking me. How could I turn religious? She was screaming. Why would a God let a wonderful, kind man like her husband suffer so and die? Why was I falling for so much stupidity? She just about threw me out of her house.

When I got back here, I told one of my friends, Rena, at *Neve* what Tzippy had said to me today. And in response, Rena just started telling me a story. She told me about a mother and father who once lived in Austria. For many years they had no children, and then when they were beginning to get old, they were finally given a son. But then one day, suddenly, their little boy got deathly ill. They were devastated. They were very poor, but they tried everything they possibly could to save their only child's life. They prayed day and night, crying by his bedside. Finally, finally, he slowly began to recover.

"Didn't you hope he would?" Rena asked me.

"Sure, why not?" I said.

"But that boy was little Adolf, and he grew up to be Adolf Hitler."

We don't see the whole picture, that's what she was trying to show me. We have very limited vision. What kind of God would I be talking about if I could understand everything that God has the capacity to understand? But even though God's understanding must be infinitely complex, I still do have to try to understand as much as I can. I have to *try* to see the bigger picture.

July 15, 1978

My dear sister Nancy,

Here I am, as usual, procrastinating writing to you. Well, I bet it's nice to know some things never change. And like we used to enjoy saying to each other, you'll always be my favorite sister!

Yes, I do know that I am hurting you by staying here. But Nancy, something very crucial was always missing for me and it would be missing in all the other professions you suggested I try, too, if the needs underneath are not met first. My constant craving for the meaning of life is not futile or ridiculous, as everyone was always telling me. I want to stop getting distracted.

But, I know, you are still asking why do I have to be in Israel? I guess it's that I want to go back to the source. I'm not so clear about this, but my feelings go something like: Why settle for the "imitation" when I can get the original here?

When I came here for the first time on a tour seven years ago, it felt so strongly like I had been here before, and that this was where I was meant to be.

Nancy, if I were to return now, it would be like you were with only the outer shell of me.

Please send me your love, although it always makes me tearful.

July 16, 1978

Dear Joanne,

I have been punctuating my summer at home with commas in Cambridge, semi-colons on Cape Cod, and periods in Vermont. I guess I am really doing nothing but odd jobs, visiting friends, writing, searching for Henry Miller's "Tropical Paradise."

What you wrote in your letter interests me because even though my mother is Jewish, I don't understand anything about Judaism. I admit, with the shamefacedness of Philip

Roth caught with chicken livers au natural, that I don't know what you mean by "jewishness." Until I was seventeen, I thought a yarmulke was a Japanese motorcycle!

Are you referring to a set of cultural rules, shall we call them rituals, by which Jews stereotypically govern their lives? I would love to know, more explicitly, what you mean. It is easy to be embarrassed about Jewishness at a place such as our alma mater, Harvard. I am skeptical, though, with too-easy labels like "Jewish."

Your letter is very much like you; timid to really come out and say it. And you always have more to say than you give yourself credit for. It is too bad we did not get to become good friends until close to graduation time. I hope this does not sound patronizing, but I am seeking a woman who is willing to give me some insights into what our pernicious society calls "the female role." There are so many games imposed on meta-games, and I am sick and tired of them. How does something like "Jewishness" come in?

Love,

Steve, your old friend from your old alma mater!

July 18, 1978

"Even Better"

How I've tried to *look* better than I am to peers,

If I'd tried to *be* better, it would have saved years.

July 23, 1978

Dear Mom and Dad,

I am trying to make myself into a more "religious" letter writer!

In the mornings I go to classes, and in the afternoons, I got a job doing physical therapy and just basic "learning and loving" work with a five-year-old girl, Debbie, who is mentally retarded and also physically handicapped. She lives just four blocks away from Neve. Right away we took to each other. She is a very tender human being, and she is trying very hard to learn new skills with me. I am learning a lot about patience. And she brings out compassion in me.

I don't think I can describe how wonderful my days are. They are filled with all the things I most love to do. It is hard for me to believe that life can be like this.

On Fridays, I help a woman with a whole bunch of children. I volunteered to watch the children and help clean their house for Shabbos each week. I am constantly astounded watching her. I'm learning a great deal from watching this woman maintain her cheerfulness and thankfulness and calm demeanor despite the never-ending commotion that goes on around her. I sure do seem to have this attraction for big families—don't I?

P.S. I just got your letter, Dad. Well now, this whole page has gotten smeared with tears. But thank you for your confidence in me. I am so lucky.

July 30, 1978

Dear Leah,

Of course, I'm scared, but it's not a vague, anxious

paralyzing fear now. It's an exhilarating one. I know it looks like I'm left with nothing. It looks like I've left myself stranded in a foreign country, where people speak a language I don't understand, without family, without friends, and without a career. And for what? Oh Leah, for everything.

There is a Jewish prayer I've started saying when I wake up in the morning. In it are words that intrigue me: "The soul which You have given me is pure."

Isn't that amazing?

I feel alone, but that's still one person more than I had along with me before. Leah, do you know what I'm thinking the purpose of life is? In a way, it is the exact opposite of what our education at Harvard taught us. It turns out that what we're really here for is to release the divine spark hidden within us. In the divine spark is every individual's greatness and uniqueness. And *that's* the inner burning we tried to extinguish all these years.

Chapter Eleven: August 10, 1978—September 22, 1978

August 10, 1978

Dear Mom and Dad,

Ben wrote me a long letter. It was great to hear from my brother-in-law, but it was disturbing to read how he feels; that I'm being influenced here too much. I wrote back to Ben already, and I will explain how I feel to you, too, now. Intellectually, I still do not accept a great deal. Much of the teaching here goes directly against a lot that I have learned throughout my life. But there's a place lodged inside—I don't know how else to explain it—where nothing has ever rung so true to me before.

There *were* elements in Buddhism, in Christian Science, in TM, even in E.S.T. that rang true to me. I tried each one, hoping it would provide the missing puzzle piece I was searching for. I tried, but they never fit exactly. I guess just because my core, my essence, is a Jewish one.

This pure form of Judaism fits. I felt the missing puzzle piece fall right into its place almost immediately. A comprehensible picture of what life is all about is finally appearing.

I can't explain why the other religions didn't fit right. I wanted them to. Maybe someday I'll understand. Maybe there really is a soul. A *neshama*, they call it here, that knows its truth when it is found. In my own backyard, that's where the answers, my buried treasure, had been hidden!

One difference between Torah Judaism and the other religions I looked into, is how questioning is encouraged.

The Jewish way is to continually struggle to see clearly what is true and good, by thinking as deeply as I have always wanted. Judaism is about digging and arguing and not accepting anything completely until it is hashed through thoroughly. Judaism almost seems to thrive on conflicting opinions. But I think other religions find them threatening. Wow! They used to tell us at E.S.T. meetings: "Don't ask why. It just works." My insides would cringe.

Do you know what is most crucial to me about Torah Judaism? I *don't* sit around and just philosophize! I also *do* specific actions. I used to love to read Hasidic tales, but I never *did* anything. It all sounded great, but I never got my body involved at all. I just sat there reading about everything and it sounded wonderful, but that was *all* I did.

I never met people actually living their lives in accordance with the Torah's directions. But the Torah is filled with specific instructions for *living*. Actions *are* critical. I've seen that it's impossible for me to be clear in my thinking, if I am not straightforward in my actions, too. Judaism addresses the needs of my whole being.

I have started to read the books of the Torah in their original Hebrew. I'm starting to see how the mysteries of the Torah are hidden in a coded form. And here I thought the Bible sounded like a book with just a lot of "begetting."

Oh Dad, you'd be especially fascinated by this. The ancient Hebrew language is a work of extraordinary genius. It's a perfectly designed system. *Literally* flawless! The twenty-two Hebrew letters are combined into three letter roots that express the *essence* of all the objects and ideas they represent. In other languages, as you know, the words are only a convention for communication. They are picked arbitrarily and they have no intrinsic connection to the things they represent. Through the language of Hebrew, the interrelationship between everything present in the world is unfolded.

And even a tiny curl at the very top of just one individual letter in the Hebrew alphabet has many levels of significance. Can you imagine? Millions of mystical messages are conveyed by the juxtaposition of the letters into words! The study of this aspect of Judaism alone could have made me do a "double-take" toward appreciating the depth of our heritage. At twenty-two years, I've found these twenty-two letters. An old language, giving my life new meaning.

Slowly but surely, I am beginning to see bits and pieces of the wisdom and the joy behind the observance of the Jewish *mitzvot*, all the Jewish guidelines. And I am starting to consider the possibility that maybe, just maybe, it is not futile to pray to God.

I always thought people prayed to be nice to God or something like that, which seemed so stupid. But now I've studied that the Hebrew word for prayer is *tefillah*, and it means "to judge oneself." The Jewish purpose of prayer is not to try to change God, but to try to change oneself, to increase our understanding of who we really are, and be honest with ourselves about our needs and our imperfections.

We hear plenty of people talk about how they "love humanity." But these same people can't even get along with their closest relatives. So, do you know what is the most amazing thing of all that I have learned? Judaism doesn't just spit out phrases that are so very easy to spit out like "be good" and "love your neighbor," it shows *how* to be good; it shows *how* to become a more loving person.

I feel that choices and decisions about my life have never come so directly from inside me as they are coming now. This is the first time I can remember consciously examining steps before I take them. What's so funny is that even with all these "laws" being presented, I really feel like *I* am actually making decisions for a change and not just flowing along with the tide. It gives me a feeling of responsibility at the same time as it gives me a taste of freedom; this new-found freedom of self-choosing!

A woman called up the school a few days ago and asked if one of the students could come to sleep at her house. She lives a few blocks away and she has become afraid to sleep alone. Her husband died recently, and she started to suffer from severe asthma attacks during the night. So I am sleeping there instead of the dorm now. But please still write to me at this same address, when you get a chance.

August 12, 1978

"Jerusalem"

Like the hills of this city,

My spirits fly up and then

Soar down.

I am getting dizzy,

Being moved about,

And with my own spinning.

I still believe that the Hand

Is gentle,

But sometimes it feels harsh.

Where's the most violent roller coaster?

In the City of Truth—no amusement park.

August 15, 1978

Dear Mom and Dad,

You wrote in the letter I just received from you, that you have heard that the rabbis here are of the "guru" style. And that the women that come here are coming out of weakness, looking for a father-figure or something. Sure, I know of several women here who come from homes without fathers. I don't think it is just coincidence that these women do seem to "guru-ize" the rabbis and talk about God as a father a lot. It makes sense that they are clinging to Judaism for that kind of support and that they are developing their relationship to God from that slant. That part I know you find understandable.

The part that is more important and maybe more difficult for you to understand is that is not the only reason that people come here. People come to find out how to live life in a Jewish way. People come in order to be able to live their lives with an understanding that God is involved throughout it. And these are usually people coming from "strong" backgrounds.

My closest friends here at the school are two social workers, a photo-journalist from the *Jerusalem Post*, and a graduate of Brandeis who was an instructor at the Harvard Graduate School of Education before coming here. I know all too well that what they are doing professionally doesn't necessarily mean that they have strong backgrounds, though. You'll have to meet them to see how lovely they are.

Anyway, I'm sure you get the point I am trying to make. Were it not for the fact that I did have a very secure upbringing, I would not be here now. I had so much love and support from both of you that I have always wanted to grow into the best possible person I could become. Before I was compromising myself away, however, on a road which to others might have appeared to be leading to the fulfillment of my greatest potential. But it was not that kind of path for me. I got lost without clear directions. Now, for the first time in such a long time, I can see the possibility for the future I have ahead of me to be both meaningful and joyful.

There is one more subject I need to bring up. Ben wrote to me, and maybe you were implying this, too, that *I* am here out of weakness. He wrote that I am here to escape from my psychological problems. He says I am running away from myself. That I am trying to sweep my issues "under the rug," but they are still there.

I don't know how to respond to this. The accusations sound so reasonable. He appears right, even to me. How could I become truly happy so quickly when I was so miserable just a short time ago? And how could I get better without confronting my problem head-on, with therapy?

I am at a loss to defend myself. I have no words to explain why I think he is wrong. It seems like what he is saying *should* be correct. And yet, somehow, it isn't.

I hope someday I'll be able to see "the bigger picture." Then I'll be able to understand how, although it appears that I am escaping here because of my weaknesses, I honestly know that this is the first move I am making with the help of a long unrecognized strength.

August 22, 1978

Dear Mom and Dad,

Yesterday the mother of the ten-year-old girl I work with in the afternoons told me that since I have been working with Debbie, it's the first time Debbie has ever slept through the night. Because her mind is truly stimulated now—and not just stimulated, but *exhausted*—when she comes back after our afternoons together. She's amazed how far Debbie has stretched out into her potential so suddenly. Her Mom said that because of Debbie sleeping at night, these past few weeks have been the first time since Debbie was born that she has been able to sleep through the whole night *herself* because Debbie is sleeping.

Also, she said that they have to get Debbie new shoes because her feet are now being stimulated by her moving more purposefully, so maybe that's why they are growing extra quickly. And then she said something else. She told me that her husband had said to her that "ever since Joanne has been working with Debbie, it is like Debbie is finally becoming a *person*!" That may sound pretty peculiar or maybe even cruel, but her father is a kind, devoted man, and he did not mean it in a cruel way at all. I understood right away what he must have meant by that for I can see Debbie's development before my eyes. I feel like I am developing so much, too, from all my afternoons out in the sunshine with Debbie. Each day it is a blessing to be alive. Each day offers me also new ways to develop into a person.

Yes, I still sleep in the house with the woman who has asthma attacks. Mostly, I think she likes having someone near her in the evenings with whom she can share her stories. She feels very alone in the world. And I like listening to the many adventures in her life.

Very tentatively, I am beginning to come away from

thinking of the whole Torah as just a classic collection of fairy tales. There are still many moments of doubt. But it is these moments *without* doubt which are new to me, and exciting.

August 30, 1978

Dear Mom and Dad,

I am really angry. I've been trying very hard to explain to you how I feel, but you continue to hold that I'm being "brainwashed by a peer-pressure group, very structured, and most influential." Really! This is *not* a group of sickeningly friendly Moonies inviting a bunch of people that look like losers in for a little food and a lot of mindless smiles. This is our *own* heritage you're talking about!

And I've got to ask you this question. How would you characterize the socialization process in which I "grew up?" There was no very influential pressure to be irreligious ever since childhood? *Come on!* I was bombarded with the strongest peer-pressure for years. Peer-pressure to go to bars, get drunk, get stoned, get boyfriends, and all of that was behind the law we all had to follow to: *Have a good time!* Do whatever you feel like doing, every man for himself, hedonism is beautiful! And you call what I am experiencing *now* peer-pressure?

The banner of the "New Religion" was waved constantly in my face. Do you think I couldn't read the words? *There are no absolutes!* And conformity was exacted in subtle ways. I accepted so many rigid dogmas unconsciously that I would never have accepted had the influences not been presented so incessantly. I didn't use my reasoning powers to check out the credibility of "the facts." I wasn't even aware that I was being influenced. Were you saying something about "brainwashing?"

You claim that observant Jews look and act like robots. All running around doing the same bunch of rituals and all dressed in the same kind of clothes. It looked that way to me too at first. But let me tell you, I burst out into a fit of laughter when it dawned on me how a collection of college kids must appear the same way. All running around doing the same bunch of rituals and all wearing the same kind of clothes. A Hasidic visitor unfamiliar with the college scene might even wonder if a plaid flannel shirt and jeans is some kind of uniform that college students have to wear.

I bet a college student would feel just about as comfortable dressing up as a Hasid on campus as a Hasid would feel dressing up like a college student in a religious neighborhood. I believed I was a pretty liberated university student, but I was actually following lists and lists of unconscious, confining rules. Unexamined commandments. The critical difference is that the observant Jew is *aware* of the rules he is following. The rules are presented *up-front*, not subliminally. And he or she is *consciously choosing* to observe them. That sounds a lot more like real freedom to me.

If I don't draw my own conclusions, I'm acting like a robot? Well, I've been a robot long enough. And it's only now that I'm beginning to catch on. A robot, robbed of my heritage, without even knowing it.

So now I'm going exploring. I'm approaching Judaism with an open mind, examining the evidence, checking out "the facts" for the very first time.

September 4, 1978

"Always Busy"

The task *is* great.

And life *is* short.

But somewhere along the way,

We get caught.

We rush and we rush,

Dash about in a tizzy,

We *must* be accomplishing,

We're *always* busy!

But we're *distracted*,

From the *task* in our haste.

We forget to *enjoy*,

So it's all a big waste.

September 10, 1978

Dear Mom and Dad,

I got a letter from the dean of the med school accepting my "taking the year off" to study here. Maybe it sounds funny to put it this way, but it's nice to know I have medical school to fall back on. Though I went to Harvard and then on to med school and was headed toward a life of which I could have felt proud, I just didn't feel proud of it. And now I see that these feelings were not unfounded. There was a much greater life in store for me.

Work with Debbie is continuing to progress beautifully. In addition to a whole repertoire of self-expression we've created using motions, she is now also beginning to communicate to me with noises. And the noises are coming closer and closer to sounding like words! It's so good that Debbie and I have each other. Together we're both starting to release what was buried inside.

Do you know what I was remembering the other day? How I used to ridicule Aunt Trudy for trying to keep a "kosher kitchen" just because she had promised her mother she would. It seemed so old-fashioned, and it embarrassed me. So I criticized her for not understanding any reasons behind that archaic tradition. Remember how I used to try to mix things up there in that kitchen just to be rebellious and show how ridiculous the whole business was?

There are still continuous arguments going on in my head. Is this really true? Am I just being duped? But as the evidence begins to add up, I am starting to prove to myself intellectually, what I grasped onto intuitively right away. There actually *may* be directions for living!

Rabbi Noach Weinberg has a funny way of putting it, "If you do believe in God and He doesn't exist, what have you lost? But if you don't believe in God and He does exist, you have everything to lose." So let's say God really exists, and He really provided us with laws of life, I should be jumping at the chance to start observing them, right? *No way!* As difficult as it is for me to synthesize these "revolutionary ideas," it is even *more* difficult to integrate the "revolutionary actions" into my already well-established behavior patterns.

In other words, my body just feels like continuing to sit here and *read* about all the beautiful principles behind the directions to eat kosher food and have a day of rest on Saturday. Action-wise, I still feel like going to the movies on *Shabbos* and eating cheeseburgers. After I've studied some of the reasons for these laws, they make so much sense to me, both intellectually and intuitively. But when I get down to actually *doing* some of these things, it's an *incredible* struggle! And do you know why it's so hard for me? I think I just figured it out. My mind is not used to exercising control over my body. My body has really been in control of my mind for years.

Imagine that! I don't want to *restrict* myself by observing the Jewish laws concerning Shabbos or the ones forbidding me to eat non-kosher food. Yet before, when I thought I could eat whatever, whenever, and whenever I felt like it, I *sure* didn't feel free.

Is it possible to break out of a negative cycle I get trapped in? Only with a positive action. So that's what Judaism is. A treasure chest stuffed with specifically designed, positive actions.

September 22, 1978

"The Women's Section"

A curtain separates.

What does that demonstrate?

We're second-rate Jews.

A curtain separates.

Who says men can dictate?

I'll sit just where I choose.

In the back of the synagogue,

They make us pray.

In the back, in the back, in the back,

They say.

In the back of the synagogue,

They make us pray.

Wake up, old men, it's a new day.

Women have equal status now.

Hold tight to your *kipas,*

You who don't allow,

Women to even sit with you.

Wake up, old men, try something new.

A curtain separates.

Must they differentiate?

They won't give us a chance.

A curtain separates.

Can I appreciate

This *quaint* experience?

O.K., I'll take a seat and see,

Just how it feels for a woman like me.

In the back, in the back, in the back, I'll be,

But I wish I could have picked this,

Independently.

It's not *so* bad to be without the men.

It's not that same old scene again.

There are less distractions, no chemistry.

There's no man to flirt with or inhibit me.

A curtain separates.

But does that demonstrate,

We're second-rate Jews?

A curtain separates.

Now I can concentrate,

Sing out the way I choose.

I look for stifled women,

But I'm the only one.

The others know the secret,

While I have just begun,

To sense the hidden power,

Of each woman in this room.

Her prayers come from the deepest place.

They pour out from her womb.

Women don't have to pray in *shul*.

Each connects to God alone.

The power of her still, small voice,

Can reach God on its own.

A curtain separates.

But it's the men it isolates,

From the power when women pray.

A curtain separates.

The power from the back -

Could just blow them away,

Blow them away…

Chapter Twelve: September 25, 1978—December 10, 1978

September 25, 1978

Dear Mom and Dad,

Standing in front of the Western Wall tonight, I had a totally new feeling. I let myself stand there, open to the possibility that God may really be hearing me.

Miracles, just superstitious folklore, invented to explain what we could not yet understand scientifically. But there I stood tonight. And felt, what a miracle.

I read recently that Galileo said, "You can't teach a person anything. You can only help him find it in himself." That must be what's happening. I could never buy the concept of a personal God. I just saw it as a crutch that some people needed to lean on so that they could go through life placated, appeased. Praying made me feel foolish. How could I pray to God to give me something, like a baby asking for a toy?

And now? Well first I think I started to give God a chance of actually being real. Very big of me. Today, I am beginning to admit that a God able to do anything, could operate on a one-to-one personal level as well as a universal one. And there is just the tiniest drop of something besides cynicism when I speak words to God out loud. Once there were so many sneering arguments going on in my head when I would try to pray that it was deafening. I could not ever hear what my heart wanted to say.

Mom and Dad, I just realized something. That it has been for me the way it has been for the Jewish people as a whole.

I remained different, no matter how hard I tried to cover up my differences and assimilate. And no matter how the Jewish people have tried to assimilate, the whole world knows that the Jews have something significantly unique.

I have heard Jewish people pointing to the Holocaust as justification for not being observant Jews. But learning about that horror has always had the opposite kind of disturbing effect on me. *Why* was it the Jewish people who were picked on as the focus of Hitler's hatred? Was it somehow *because* Judaism gave humanity the concept of one God, justice, democracy, universal peace, and dignity of the individual, just to mention a few? Why, the Jewish people even gave the world J.C.! Do we have some kind of consciousness about us, maybe, that Hitler didn't want to have to face? Something he wanted to erase forever?

We're really such a *small* group of people. And yet how come we're so disproportionately involved in international conflicts? Even when I take a look at the geniuses who most affected changes in 20th Century thinking, it's us Jews again, Freud, Marx, Einstein. What's going on? Something *must* be going on.

Tonight when I came back from the Western Wall, I sat out on the balcony and read over my journal. I read what I had written just before I ended up going to my first class at this school: "Ten years have gone away from the time when I first began wondering about the purpose of life...I haven't gotten any answers I could live with." Just a little while ago, I couldn't see any other way to get out of the fast lane, besides giving up completely and just letting myself crash.

Was it really just a short while ago? Faint glimmers of light in other religions and in diluted forms of Judaism were all I had to lead me to continue to search through the dark for something greater. But now it is as if the veil that made everything in life appear pointless and valueless was simply lifted. Suddenly, the world is restored right before my eyes in its full beauty. And I can even make trite remarks like that, and not feel ashamed.

Yes, I have found what I have been looking for, but it feels familiar. I really feel like I am coming back to something, that I once knew, but lost.

September 27, 1978

Dear Kathy,

I hope your second year of medical school is off to a good start. It wasn't easy for me to decide not to come back this year, but it was the right decision.

I am sorry I haven't written. You'll understand why I put it off. But I can't put it off anymore. Before *Yom Kippur*, Jews do an "inner accounting." We try hard to face ourselves, and especially focus on all that we have done in the past year. But before we ask God for forgiveness, we need to try to make amends if we can, and ask forgiveness from all the people we remember hurting.

Here is the money I have earned from the part-time job I have, looking after a child. It is to cover all the food that I took from you. And it uncovers what I did.

It probably seems strange to you that I want to ask for forgiveness, even though you would never find out that I was the culprit without my admitting it to you right now. I have no acceptable excuse to give you for what I did. I was in a lot of pain. I hope somehow you will be able to forgive me.

Yes, I was the Mysterious Salami Stealer, and the one who stole *all* the food that was missing last year.

October 8, 1978

Dear Mom and Dad,

It is the day before the Jewish Festival of *Sukkot*. And it looks like a glorious, colorful circus is taking place in the streets! All the people are bustling about, hurrying to buy lots of simple goodies for the holiday.

There are so *many* children here (because the observant Jews generally have large families) and they are all excitedly scurrying about; older ones taking care of the younger brothers and sisters. The main avenue is suddenly filled with makeshift vendors, displaying flowers, plants, fruit, ribbons, streamers, and all kinds of bright and shiny *Sukkah* decorations. The beggars are all out, too, wishing everyone a good, sweet new year and a happy holiday. It's kind of hard to walk through the streets, but I surely don't care. I'm not in any hurry at all anymore. I'm just absorbing the whole lively scene, taking it all in. How I love being a part of all this!

Did I write you yet that Debbie's parents have decided to put her in a full-day special education school now? She made so much progress that her whole prognosis has been revised and they have hope for their daughter again. This will be our last week of afternoons together. I guess we will have to figure out some way to express "good-bye."

I am beginning to think about how much I would love to be a mother someday. And I've also been thinking about the kind of qualities I am looking for in a husband. It is an extremely different sort of person than I would have looked for just a few short months ago. I have gone out with several men that I've been introduced to, and I'm enjoying this whole discovery process.

October 15, 1978

"Fragile Wings"

Where was the freedom promised?

Where was the open sky?

Hello, now meet the prisoner,

Who thought that she could fly.

Religious girls in summer,

Blouses buttoned up high.

I'd see long skirts with stockings,

As I would pass them by.

I'd laugh inside me, mocking,

Those girls I used to see.

Those girls are missing so much.

How trapped could people be?

But how could I have known then,

Jogging through summer rain?

I strode past them, uncovered,

In years before the pain.

Those girls kept their wings hidden,

And my own wings got crushed.

Why did I jump too quickly?

Why was my childhood rushed?

Crystalline wings they treasured,

Even at that young age.

I found my wings were fragile,

When I hit bars within this cage.

My wings have long been broken.

Can they still be healed?

Those girls now fly past rainbows.

Tell me—how does it feel?

Inside, I'm thrashing lamely.

Can I get free?

Now I can see the picture,

Reversed ironically.

October 24, 1978

Dear Mom and Dad,

One day during *Sukkot*, I ate a meal with the family I help on Fridays. In their *sukkah*, I met a man they know who studies at another school for "late beginners" in Torah Judaism, similar to the one I attend. His name is Dan and I liked him right away. He is from Oregon, and he is an architect. He's twenty-seven, and he started becoming religious about three years ago.

He is a very strong, stable kind of person. There is an openness and warmth to him. His feet are on the ground, but I know he can fly, too.

November 11, 1978

Dear Mom and Dad,

Dan and I have been seeing a lot of each other. You know in these circles, when men and women spend time together, they don't have to waste a lot of time "playing games." Both the women *and* the men *actually* share the same goal: to find a life time partner. What a switch that is from what I'd gotten used to. It is such a liberating feeling to be able to be myself finally with a man. We both want to be as honest with each other as we can be. Because we both need to have clarity to make one of the most important choices there is.

Did I ever tell you Dan's reaction when I first told him that I had gone to Harvard? There wasn't any. He had no reaction. He went right on to another subject after I told him, and I figured he couldn't possibly have heard what I said. I mean, everyone is always so blown away when I tell them where I went to college. So I actually said again, "Did you hear me say I went to Harvard?"

"Yeah, why?" he asked.

"Doesn't that *mean* anything to you?" I tried.

"What should it mean?" he asked me, genuinely puzzled.

He wasn't feeling shocked or defensive or inferior to me because of it. He didn't have any of the insecure male reactions I always received when I'd mention Harvard. It really means nothing to him. And for some reason, though I'm not exactly sure why, that means an awful lot to me.

November 13, 1978

Dear Joanne,

My life is upside down. I am trying to understand what I want. I've been working as a grill cook at the Rendezvous, which you may recall is the restaurant between Elsie's and Gino's near Harvard Square. I am seeing a psychiatrist at Cambridge Community Hospital. It is helpful in getting me to see what it is that I carry around with me, imposing on the world I see.

The relationship between myself and Lisa has ended. I was having a hard time in many ways, and she also had much to deal with. Both of us had little energy to spare.

I am very self-involved. I miss you still.

Michael

November 14, 1978

To: Rabbi Stanley Schwartz, Hillel Director

Dear Rabbi Schwartz,

You gave me answers that let me walk away guilt-free. I

could be a Jew, but that need not interfere with my life. Why couldn't you have told me that my Jewish soul was very strong, yet very fragile? That I had to tend it carefully for it to thrive? You told me I could marry a Catholic, act like I'm not Jewish, not believe in God, and still be a Jew, but it bothered me. What would it mean then?

You never helped me understand why I was living, but you *were* good at telling jokes. Do you really think young Jews will want to stay if you just make it all sound easy?

Rabbi Schwartz, if a young Jewish woman should come to you with her important questions again, tell her the truth you *know* is truth is in those moments when you face yourself. Don't try to sell her a good bargain that isn't worth much.

Sincerely,

Bracha

(My *Hebrew* name is Bracha, but you knew me as Joanne.)

December 5, 1978

Dear Mom and Dad,

Do you know what Dan is like? All the boring, stable, "nice Jewish guys" you always wanted me to date. Except he's exciting. And I think I understand why. Our *neshamas* get on great together. Our souls connect. That makes all the difference.

We share such similar values and goals. Even our backgrounds are alike. We're both from middle-class, Conservative-Jewish homes. Now his parents live in Oregon, but *get this*: he was actually born in Queens, too, on Saunders Street, two blocks away from *our* apartment building! And *here* we had to meet, *half a world away!* What do you think that could mean? I'm not sure myself!

You know, with all the "games" eliminated, you can get to understand another person deeply and honestly, very quickly. There's no "monkey business" before or outside of marriage. We don't even *touch* each other. Well, not physically, anyway. But I think that's why we are able to touch each other within, that much more sensitively.

It is, surprisingly, such a freedom, not to have to get involved physically right away. Being free to get to know Dan in every other way, first. All the other aspects of a person besides their outer image become that much more vibrant.

December 10, 1978

From the book, *A Tzaddik in Our Time,* page 150:

One of his students, of marriageable age, was about to embark on the seas of matrimony. So he came to Reb Aryeh and asked, "How should I behave toward my wife? How should I treat her?"

Reb Aryeh looked at him in wonder. "How can you ask a question like that? A wife is like your own self. You treat her as you treat yourself."

And indeed, when his own good wife, Hannah, felt pains, he went with her to Dr. Nahum Kook and told him, "My wife's foot is hurting us…"

To a young Talmud scholar who was recently wed, the good rabbi gave this prescription: It is a *mitzvah*, a precept of the Torah that a man shall make his wife happy

(Deuteronomy 24:5)...So it is necessary to behave in a way that will blend respect with love and intimacy so that nothing will interfere between (a husband and wife), just as nothing interferes between one's right and left hands, since they are both part of him...

When he leaves the house, he should tell his wife where he is going. When he comes back, he should tell her where he was and what he did, and so with all little matters like that. For the purpose of all this is to strengthen the bond between them, to reinforce their love and cheer the heart...

When his oldest grandson was about to marry, he gave him this advice: When you come home, do not go and leave things strewn on the bed, for your wife (and children) to clear away. Do not impose on her that she should serve you needlessly.

Chapter Thirteen: 1979—1982

January 1, 1979

Dear Mom and Dad,

I know last night's phone conversation was kind of a shock for you. I only wish you could see how I'm glowing through and through. I wanted to tell you some more about our engagement last night.

We were standing in front of The Western Wall. It was the last night of Chanukah, so all eight torches were lit on the giant *Menorah* at The Wall. The flames formed flickering shadows that were dancing all over us, while we talked.

On Chanukah, the Temple was re-dedicated, after the ancient Greeks and their defilements were removed from it. Chanukah is a time when the potential for re-dedication is great. And on the eighth night, that potential is the greatest of all.

We dedicated our lives to each other too, last night. I am praying that our life together will always be radiant with light, like that *Menorah* was, and *lasting,* like the Western Wall that witnessed our engagement.

January 3, 1979

Dear Mom and Dad,

You had this rabbi call me up from New York and tell me to break off my engagement. You told him I'm involved in some cult and I'm so weak, they are forcing me to marry someone I don't even know.

I am furious. But, oh God, I also understand how you must be feeling. I really do. I mean, you're so far away, and many changes have happened in my life very quickly. So you want me not to go ahead and get married too fast.

How could I possibly explain why you can trust me? I mean I'm afraid of making such a big decision, but I feel ready for it, almost over-ready.

I want someone to give to deeply. I feel so much inside that I want to start to give in an enduring relationship. I want to begin a family. Dan is a very loyal and caring kind of person, and what I see most clearly of all his traits is that he has a good heart.

Mom and Dad, somehow try to think of all the things you love in me, and hard as it is, trust my insight now.

January 9, 1979

Joanne,

I have been writing this letter mentally for five months without success. How can I know what, or if, you think of me now? I suspect my name lies buried in your list of former non-Jewish boyfriends, perhaps distinguished as the only Southern Baptist among the collection.

I could write of my life at med school. But to one preoccupied with monumental problems of religion and mankind, that would seem trivial. (By the way, what *is* the meaning of life?)

I did gain much from knowing you, and I invite you to drop by the next time you visit South Carolina. Probably, this invitation will go unanswered.

I apologize for not realizing how miserable you were here. Keep in touch.

Bill McDonald

January 21, 1979

Dear Leah,

They threw a surprise engagement party for me at *Neve*, and my friends put on a little skit about the changes in my life. One woman was dressed up as my mother and another one was supposed to be me. At the end, "my mother" turns to "me" and says, "We wanted you to marry someone Jewish, but *this* is *ridiculous*!"

I had to send you this quick postcard.

Wishing you were here,

Joanne

March 17, 1979

"Dancing"

I know this song sounds simple,

But that's all I want to say,

Thank You, God, for how my life has gone.

That's all I feel today.

Discos, wild parties, crazy nights,

Crowded bars with the dimmest lights.

I've got the right top, I've got the right pants.

Don't hold back now—just dance, dance, dance!

Isn't this fun? It's *got* to be!

Maybe there's something wrong with me.

At night everyone got so stoned.

How come I just felt so alone?

Aw—don't leave now—we've just begun.

Come on, let loose and have some fun.

With them—I pretend—but with me—I can't.

Why am I so different?

I could have just gone on that way.

No morals left, the world drained gray.

I'd still be dancing all night long,

To the same loud bands and the same loud songs.

Dizzy and scared, wishing to be found,

But no way to get off that merry-go-round.

I walk out from the *chuppah*,

A wave of love surrounds.

My friends and family all join hands.

I'm twirling round and round.

Who would have believed,

I could feel pure once more?

This woman had given up,

Just one year before.

I know this song sounds simple,

But that's all I want to say.

Thank You, God, for how my life has gone.

That's all I feel today.

April 5, 1979

Dear Leah,

Thank you so much for your wedding present. That big, beautiful photo of the Harvard Commons at night, is already hanging up in our living room.

To keep you posted on what's been happening, a few days before the wedding, March 25, my parents arrived in Israel. I didn't realize that they had come with the hope of stopping me from getting married.

It was very difficult, to say the least, listening to them discourage me from marrying Dan, nearly every waking minute. I was a wreck. Then, the day before the wedding, they took me to see a Dr. David Weiss. He is the head of the Department of Oncology at Hadassah Hospital, the one who had helped my mother get the volunteer job at Hadassah for me last summer. I guess my Mom hoped that he'd "come through" for her again. This was their last-ditch effort to still try and "rescue" me.

But to everyone's surprise, after my parents told the Chief of Oncology my story, he responded, "Many bright young Jewish people are becoming doctors today. But how many have the spark of Judaism still burning within them? How many are there who are able to try to do something to stop Judaism from being destroyed?" It was just about the last thing *any* of us expected to hear. And it certainly put a lid on things for a while, thank God.

Now, do you want to hear about the wedding, since you couldn't be there? Well, I'll tell you, it was a taste of what heaven must be like, but also hell in that my mother wore sunglasses throughout the wedding; she was crying the entire time.

Now for the part that was like heaven. Under the *chuppah*. I walked in a circle around Dan seven times, surrounded by candlelight. I did not feel like I was on earth. The family problems just floated up, under all the stars out that night over Jerusalem. I was really trying to talk to God the whole time I was under that *chuppah*. God's Presence felt closer to me than ever under there. I prayed for everyone I had ever known. And it is said that the *neshamas* of all the children you will ever have are present there, too, at your *chuppah*. Oh God, I felt them there, Leah. I really did. They were all smiling and beautiful.

I've got to tell you about one other spectacular moment. After the glass was broken and everyone shouted, "*Mazel Tov!*" and we came out from under the *chuppah*, and everyone ran to us, singing and dancing, Dan's hand reached out and found mine.

How can I explain it, Leah? Those strong, yet hesitant fingers. It was the most sensual experience in my life, our two hands touching. Finally letting ourselves join each other physically. And Leah, I felt innocent that first night. Innocent and happy, like a woman who had never *ever* been touched before.

November 2, 1979

Dear Leah,

Well, I'm pregnant. But it's no picnic. I am nauseous and exhausted all day long. For months I've done nothing but sleep. I just keep falling back to sleep all the time. Is this what a semi-comatose state is like?

Dan came home one night and asked, "Where's dinner?"

Dinner!" I shrieked, with the only energy I had left, *"I did the laundry today!"*

I had a job working at a nursing home in the recreational therapy department, but I started to get nauseous and horribly tired while working. I didn't know what was wrong with me, but I had to quit. Nobody ever told me pregnancy was like this! But then again, nobody ever told me a lot of things.

It's so hard to remember that I'm not just lying around here like a drip, doing nothing. I'm really helping create another human being. *Boy*, is that hard to believe.

It's so different than when I was studying at *Neve*. There I was studying the Torah most of the day and it was easy to stay focused on priorities. Yes, I believe that the Torah contains good directions for living. But now it is a struggle to stay on course. I thought I was such a great person while I was in *Neve*. I was sure I was going to save the world. And now, just going down the block to buy groceries and coming back in a good mood is a big accomplishment.

And, I don't know, questions about the woman's role in Judaism are bothering me. All this woman's work/man's work dichotomy, *is* it just to keep women in their place, just some brainwashing material they've been feeding us? Sometimes it's as clear as the sickeningly slick shine on my newly washed floors: a woman's work is what a man doesn't want to do. All these women I see around me in the neighborhood here—perpetually pregnant, surrounded by crying babies, doing tons of housework—am I supposed to believe that they are really happy?

December 5, 1979

Her problem

Was that the

Four walls wouldn't

Talk back to her.

That could all be changed

By installing

An echo system.

January 25, 1980

Laundries hanging on the lines,

Some birds are passing through.

When will I learn

The answer won't appear

In neon lights on Broadway.

I have to make my own heart stir.

March 8, 1980

"Now it's Our Turn"

A righteous Jew.

We have the chance

To help create one.

To let him see

Why he was born

From the very start.

Not after twenty years

Groping through confusion

Like we did.

From the beginning

We can sing him

The eternal song,

Yet can we teach him, too,

Our joy of newness,

When he'll have Torah

All along?

We must live

So carefully.

To deserve this

Sacred birth.

It will not be easy

To always remember

What it is worth.

The chance is thrilling.

We have so much to learn.

Can you believe it? With our coming baby –

Now, it's our turn.

April 15, 1980

"Advance Notice"

To Whom It May Concern,

Let me tell you a secret: Whenever your mother acts
grouchy and lazy and fed-up and nasty, and you get the
feeling that she has had *enough* of your endless crying and

whining, just remember what I am letting you know *before* you even show up:

You are doing more for her than anyone else could. You are transforming this die-hard taker into a giver.

And that's what I've wanted all along.

June 2, 1980

"A Painless Delivery"

The hell that could have been,

sliding back fast

as they put me under

and I am no longer the one

in charge of my life.

Injected with drugs,

the jumps are wild, broken

all

nightmares glare at me

vividly.

why in my most present moment

in the world

bringing warmth out -

they've stopped me cold.

Right

as I am choosing life

- this life,

I am reminded, pulled

into my past.

Groping out into contrast.

Here, in the clearing mist,

Appreciation getting born -

The hell that could have been.

April 18, 1981

Today I did nothing

But wipe my child's nose,

Hold her head as she threw up,

Then changed all her clothes.

When she *was* feeling better,

Fixed her a good meal.

Today I got nothing done,

Just something *real*.

December 2, 1982

"Between the Braids"

What's in the spaces between the braids
Of these new challahs I just made?
How much of me is hidden there?
Between the braids my thoughts appear.

First I sifted the flour through,
Thinking of what else I could do.
Who wants to be here, baking bread?
I could write my first book instead.

I added each ingredient,
And wondered why my soul was sent.
I cracked two eggs, and then two more.
Is this what I was created for?

"Shabbos Kodesh…Shabbos Kodesh,"
My lips whisper, hands knead the dough.
Let me see my work is holy,

Raising high what seems so low.

Does the challah absorb frustration?

Does the challah hear my voice, so shrill?

Does the challah absorb my confusion,

As it rises for hours on the windowsill?

I've heard that Sarah, our first mother,

Once had the right recipe.

What happened to it through the years?

Is there a copy left for me?

Stuck here in the kitchen,

And still longing for fame.

When did simple giving

Get such a bad name?

"Shabbos Kodesh…Shabbos Kodesh,"

Open up my eyes.

Let me see my work is holy.

Let me stop chasing lies.

On Friday night, my husband

Makes a blessing, and I know

Just what's inside those challahs,

Though I wouldn't tell him so.

He cuts them up, we eat them,

And I can't help but smile,

For all that work, I used to think,

They last such a short while.

But this time I see what's left,

I know what's hidden there.

In the empty spaces between the braids -

That's where my thoughts appear.

When every crumb has vanished

From the challahs that I made,

What will remain?

Just my secret struggles.

Offered up between the braids.

December 8, 1983

Dear Ruth, Mary Sue, and Barbara,

Thank you for sending me the new edition of the book,

Women Look at Biology Looking at Women. I enjoyed it and I think the collection of articles have been improved since I last saw them.

Now that I have been studying a little bit about Judaism though, I realize that Paula's article contains misinformation on the Jewish laws of *niddah* (the period of time around a woman's menstrual cycle when husbands and wives refrain from intimate relations). The *niddah* phase is a time that points up so clearly that intimate relations are only one aspect of the male-female relationship. It makes it clear that a woman should not be regarded as a sexual object. It demonstrates that there are countless abilities within a woman beside her reproductive and sexual ones. And the *niddah* guidelines emphasize that this fact must be acknowledged by men.

The relationship between Orthodox men and women obviously changes during the *niddah* period. For men who were not originally raised as Orthodox Jews, it is a real eye-opening experience. A time for learning about the wider scope of what being a woman means. The narrow view from which they were "programmed" to peer at women nearly all their lives, gets stretched.

Translating the woman's state during the *niddah* phase as being "unclean" and all terminology describing the *niddah* period as a "disgraceful" time for Jewish women are products of ignorant "macho" views. These views have crept in, I feel, in order to undermine the *niddah* concept. And it is not surprising that *chauvinistic* males would like to denigrate the whole notion of *niddah*. But as we feminists know well, just because ignorant views are rampant (with a considerable distortion of the actual facts, of course) does not mean that those "unclean" views are justified or correct.

In addition, I would like to mention that in the article, "Taking the Men Out of Menopause," the authors write about the Jewish mother, without even putting it in quotation marks, or preferably, stating instead "the *sterotypic* version of the Jewish mother." As is, it is anti-Semitic slander. *Even* if the authors of the article are Jewish. Believe me, I know that it is possible to be both Jewish and anti-Semitic. I spent years of my life that way.

A domineering, guilt-inflicting "yenta" is a woman missing Torah guidelines and values. The stereotype is a *warped* martyr, a *phony* giver—the direct opposite of what the true pillars of this community are like.

December 26, 1983

"Wonder Girl"

My whole life I've been waiting for applause,

Neon lights, autographs, Nobel Prize.

My whole life I've been waiting for applause.

When it comes, I'll act coy and surprised.

Secretly I've waited, always wanting to believe

That the applause would never stop after I'd achieve.

Secretly I've waited, always wanting to believe

What an elusive tapestry a mixed up mind can weave.

I worked hard so that I could reach the top,

A Harvard grad, with A's on every test.

I worked hard so that I could reach the top,

The world would know—it would show—I was best.

So why'd it always happen I could not convince myself?

Awards just made a hollow sound when placed upon the
shelf.

And why'd it always happen that the praises stopped so
fast?

Isn't there a goal to reach where my glory will last?

Then one day I got tired of this game.

Wonder girl, though you've won, what's it worth?

Then one day I got tired of this game.

Craving more, is it found, here on earth?

Well, it has not been easy putting old wishes aside.

While washing piles of dishes, my hands burn with
swallowed

pride.

No, it has not been easy putting old wishes aside.

Though I have young children now, the old dreams never
died.

This afternoon it was raining very hard.

My little ones were getting bored—nowhere to go.

This afternoon it was raining very hard.

I decided to put on a puppet show.

Lining up their kiddie chairs, they sat there in a row.

I peeked out at them a moment, and their faces were aglow.

Lining up their kiddie chairs, they sat there in a row.

Their eyes were full of wonder, as they watched my puppet show.

My whole life I've been waiting for applause.

Well, it came. And it's true. It was great.

My whole life I waited for *this* applause.

Their little hands, clapping for joy, were worth the wait.

And suddenly I realized that here within these walls,

I did something much greater than in all the lecture halls.

Suddenly I realized that *this* glory does not leave.

Strand by strand, elusive tapestries are starting to unweave.

Chapter Fourteen: 1983—1985

January 26, 1983

Dear Barbara,

I was glad you responded in such a positive way to my letter about the book. I honestly didn't expect it. Sure, I have a lot more thoughts that I'd be very happy to share with you. Years ago, when we were working on the feminist critique together, you were Jewish *and* you were angry, but what could I say to you then? What can I say to you now…when I have this chance?

You seemed to hate men vehemently at the time. They were the ones who had put you down, kept you "in your place" for all these millennium. It was *their* fault. That was so clear to you. Remember how we all used to hang out in Bread and Roses restaurant—all the angry feminists of Radcliffe, who were mostly Jewish, and who could see so clearly that men were the culprits and that women had been the victims. I was there, too, but if you remember, I never had much to say at any of our meetings. I didn't see it all so clearly. Something bothered me with all this talk about the good guys and the bad guys…and most of all…it seemed so full of anger.

Now here I am, seven years later, finally feeling ready to say something back to you. What I have to say will sound strange at first, I know, and that is why a part of me doesn't even want to bother. At the same time, I know it is important for me to let you hear my thinking now.

Remember the disgust we used to feel when we were considered nothing but bodies by all those men out there?

Those were our souls reacting. When we were striving to be treated with the same respect that men were afforded, when we were fighting to have the opportunity to fulfill our greatest potentials as women—and even when society's stress on skin-surface beauty was making us sick deep down inside—*all* of those times—it was our Jewish *neshamas* (souls) that were crying out to be recognized by us.

I know what you'd think of me if you saw me. Not usually barefoot, but pregnant and baking bread (*challahs*) on a regular basis. Right away you would probably classify me as one of those who had given up. But it's more the other way around. I turned away from all the anger at Bread and Roses because it was on a dead-end street. All I knew then was that it couldn't be the way for us to get somewhere.

Last time we saw each other, I was headed for medical school in South Carolina. The summer after my first year there, I took a trip to Israel. I had just six weeks of vacation until my second year of medical school would begin. I was coming in search of something that was missing in life, and I knew that this was the last stop I was going to make before resigning myself completely to the cynical, de-sensitized way of life I was finally getting used to. I could not understand at the time that the constant, un-surrendering force inside that kept pushing me onward and wouldn't let me rest was Jewish. The drive to meet our spiritual needs is in all of us, but we don't usually recognize where the deep and unfulfilled cravings are coming from.

We had dismissed Judaism early on, as being unable to provide any solutions to the problems that were important to us. The graduation ceremonies from Judaism were held at gaudy Bar Mitzvah receptions. There was more than plenty of good food, but nothing that lasted. Then later on, we all heard stuff about how the status of a woman was inferior to that of a man's in Judaism. Someone once even showed us some Jewish laws to prove it. We didn't hear much, but what we did hear made a lot of sense. After all, it was exactly what we had suspected.

Well, now I wish I could ask you to take a second look. I would ask you to look from the place that lies even deeper than your anger. From that pure part of you still unmarred from long years of hating. I want you to look at me and see what there is to this woman that you would find doing dishes, changing diapers, and making dinner for her husband every day. You never wanted others to judge you at face value. Now, I'm asking for that, too.

An understanding of the woman's true role in Judaism can only be obtained by suspending your usual way of thinking for a while. From the very start, we have been taught to believe that public recognition is what counts. We saw men out up front in prestigious positions getting a lot of recognition, and we wanted it too. It seemed to those lurking in the background that men were having all the fun, living life in the most exciting way.

But who told us that out in public is "where the action is"? Who was telling us that success in the public arena would make us happy? And who got us thinking that being a homemaker was a drag? What I'm trying to say is somewhere along the line most of us accepted an assumption which no one ever proved to us. We believed it when "they" told us that getting public recognition would bring fulfillment, and yet we never even saw one living example of it.

In these intervening years, through exploring authentic Judaism, I've had the chance to discover a fact of life that was never disclosed to me before. Simply put: What's up front is not what counts. It's still very hard for me to accept that thoroughly, however. It will take a long time for me to adjust to this view of life, completely topsy-turvy to the one I'd been indoctrinated to hold up until then.

In a sense, though, I think this topsy-turvy view of what really matters in life can be considered a truly feminist way of thinking. It requires recognizing fully that the man's role is not the preferred role. Once this readjustment in thinking can be integrated at a deep level within, it finally becomes possible for a woman to realize her greatest potential. Once freed from the burden of wanting to be like a man, she is able to be a woman wholeheartedly. We are then able to taste the many pleasures inherent in creating a home. These are pleasures of the deepest sort, which we would have never even permitted ourselves to accept and experience as pleasures before.

I am a pioneer woman now. We have left Jerusalem to begin a new settlement in the Judean desert. Here I am, sitting in front of my small caravan house. My view is of the hills of Judea, stretching out to the Dead Sea. The wide open spaces here have helped open me. I have room to grow, to stretch out into myself. And this horizon gives encouragement. I think I love these barren hills because their potential is so awesome. Though it looks impossible at this very minute, soon they, too, will burst forth with life.

My two children, Elana and Dovid, are taking naps right now. I can't wait 'til they wake up and I can feel their little bodies, warm from sleep, and see those beautiful faces of theirs again. And yet I remember clearly how terrified I was when I found out that I was pregnant for the first time. I had no idea what to do with an infant. In fact, I didn't even like babies. And at the thought of that never-ending responsibility, I envisioned my freedom leaving forever.

A new level of freedom was first given to me three years ago, when Elana, my first child was born. From the moment

I held her soft little body and kissed it—when we first met in the hospital—I could truly feel deep levels within me opening up, becoming freed for the first time.

My head had certainly not been filled with gushy-mushy thoughts about the joys of becoming a mother before Elana was born. It had been filled with terror. The tenderness that poured out when I felt that warm life force breathing beside me was as real me as could be, though. Something at my core was definitely released. New parts have been awakening ever since.

I'm not trying to say that in order for every Jewish woman's *neshama* to achieve fulfillment, she has to be a full-time homemaker. What I believe is that we have to be open to enable the spiritual nourishment that we all need to get in. When creating a holy environment in which love can grow is a woman's top priority, the spiritual nourishment gets through in a steady flow.

I'm also not trying to say that every minute as a Jewish homemaker has been a delight. I mean, it could have been if I had let it—but some old thoughts still hold me down. There are times when I wish that my children would just leave me alone and let me do what I "feel like doing". But then they *are* there, wanting me to read to them, feed them, or simply hold them. And *boy* does that push me to grow in ways that I never would have been able to before. Then there is my husband. It is even harder to be giving to him. I hear all these old whispers when I am doing things for him. I bet they're coming from brain cells still lodged in there since Bread and Roses. "What are you, his *servant*?" or "Men! They're all alike!" those brain cells hiss, and sometimes I succumb.

It's pretty futile to try to argue with these subliminal voices directly. They'll say something that still stings, and then fade away with a mocking, condescending laugh. The best way for me to quiet that kind of irritating chatter is for me to fill my mind with higher things. Little by little, as I learn more about myself, more about what the purpose of life is, and more about which pleasures in life are the greatest and most lasting, the resentful voices slink away, ineffective.

One of the biggest obstacles we have to get beyond is that we've actually been taught to see giving in a negative light. Our secular training tells us that it's the women who are the givers and the men who are the traditional takers. I don't understand why this creates anger, though, since God, the One we all seek to emulate, is universally recognized as the Ultimate Giver. Still, I wish I could somehow get you to come and visit with families whose homes are built solidly upon a Torah base. Both the men and the women are clearly trained from the very start of their lives to strive to become givers. In fact, a man gets married, according to Torah opinion, so that he will have the opportunity to give during the course of his life in the most significant way.

The role of the Jewish people is to make clear the spiritual essence of every single physical entity in this world. A Jewish woman can choose to be at the very center of this most holy work. We are the ones who largely determine whether or not the spiritual potential inherent in all things will be brought out. Seemingly mundane actions are transformed into uplifting, limitlessly inspiring experiences when a Jewish woman's body and soul move in sync, with clarity.

Now, how do I feel about housework? How do I feel selling my mind away for several hours each day, you are probably wondering? That was another one of my big fears. I was terrified that housework would destroy my brain. It is still a shock to me to find that, in actuality, the opposite process is occurring. I can feel myself developing a finer tuning to life. When I am focused on the ultimate goal of my work, then every small action I take becomes elevated. What is my job? To try to elicit the spiritual essence of each person and each thing I touch.

Maybe it will be helpful to explain it this way. Let's say a woman spends hours on end doing things like sewing, scrubbing, wiping up bruises, washing off parts of the body that are "usually not exposed," practicing a pleasant bedside manner, etc. It would sound like such stupid, boring work to me. But if I realized that that woman was a brain surgeon, I would see it all differently. Individual actions only appear mundane when we don't understand the greater purpose behind them.

Torah-observant women really are happy in this life. I can't get over it. Watching a mother of ten fluidly move through her day is the most beautiful ballet I ever watched.

It just keeps shocking me, knocking over nearly everything I learned for nearly twenty years. *How could it be that my days are exciting?* Here I am with as close up a view as possible and I still can't accept it. There were all those years of being more than sure that this work was degrading, stifling, maddening. But if I completely forget the negative view of being a traditional Jewish homemaker for just one moment, I am left with only joy. I'm still washing the same dishes, but within a world immersed in wonder.

How did it happen that I began to see it really was a great life for me and the other women, trying to lead our lives according to the Torah's guidelines? I gave it a little chance, I guess. You mean, maybe we're not all playing some pathetic game, trying to fool ourselves and fool each other? You mean, we're not just trying to convince ourselves that this way of life makes sense? You mean, we're not all just *pretending* to be happy? We really *are*? But that's so *simple*! Who could believe it? Since I was trained to appreciate that appearances are what count, it was hard to understand that there is a different set of rules being used here. It was difficult for me to trust that these women were not being phony when they said how sweet their lives were. It was difficult for me to trust them because being phony had become "second nature" to me.

I thought men must have just gotten a lot of female Orthodox *schnooks* to go around and say how great their role was. All those pregnant women with nine children I saw, crowded into their tiny apartments, I could have *sworn* they had to be suffering. My imagination couldn't stretch far enough to even *conceive* of their being happy.

Whenever a voice inside wants me to look at the negative side of things, it can go on and on and get convoluted this way and swerve around that way and go dashing down every dark alley in order to explain things. But when another voice wants me to see the goodness in life, it just speaks directly, in a deep, clear tone. I used to think all the sophisticated cynics knew more than me, back when I was still looking at everything naively and simply. Then, after I became skillful at seeing the world cynically, I found out that 'simple' and 'good' actually is the way life's meant to be. With just the right soundtrack playing in the background, this would be the kind of life so many would be after.

Is it just that the "brainwashing" finally got to me? Or maybe it's only that the previous years of brainwashing are beginning to wear off? So, I am re-evaluating every aspect of my new way of life throughout each day. Can this be "brainwashing" if there is critical analysis going on constantly? My sophisticated education has left me more reluctant than others, I guess, to accept simple truths. But I've seen too much powerful evidence by now to let my entire scope of vision remain clouded any longer. I know it's a wonderful life. It is sweetly good and, when I'm aware, it is *cosmicly* good. I can fly into spiritual ecstasy while my feet are planted on the linoleum floor and my hands are still dusty with flour and smelling like Desitin.

Sure, I'm annoyed at times when the babies are cranky and I can't sit down. I may want to just read a certain article, but I can't. Then the pangs of annoyance subside, and I'm able to rise above them and see what's beyond; what the larger picture of life looks like and the kind of person I want to become. I see that there is a growth going on that no article I would have read during that same time could have given me. I am expecting, God willing, my third child soon. When I found out that I was pregnant for this third time, would you believe, *once again*, those old fears flashed through me. *Now all my freedom will surely be gone,* I worried. But what is freedom, if not having the opportunity to achieve one's potential? And what career would I prefer to have? What other career can be compared with this most intimate cultivation of real-life masterpieces?

I can't begin to imagine what this next child will bring into my life, and add to the world. I know that there must be a great deal that I need to receive from his or her unique source.

Does my being a woman devoted to creating a truly Jewish home still make me seem like some kind of martyr to you? But a martyr to what? Really, when you think about it, what am I sacrificing? Am I sacrificing myself to become a better person? What am I losing? Can you imagine how much there is to be gained?

If you want to know about a time when I felt that a great deal of my potential *was* withering away, I could tell you about how I felt during my first year of medical school. Essential parts of me were suffocating through the desensitization process required there. But that's me.

In order to be an observant Jewess, a woman does not have to be a full-time homemaker. I think it *is* a wonderful option, though, for a mother with young children. It is an option which has been unfairly denigrated, if not virtually obliterated as a vitally worthwhile option. The choice to be home with one's children is also considered, undeservedly, to be economically unfeasible. Leading a simple, spiritual life, however, is a very viable and healthful choice, which is not given due consideration.

One last thing I want to ask you. Have you ever wondered about how Judaism has managed to be preserved through thousands of years? I think the answer is: what is most sacred about it, its greatest treasures, are not left out for public display. We turned away from Judaism when we were both in college. But we had actually never even met Judaism, only some very cheap imitations of it. And yet, that is exactly what has been its protection device. In order to get at the core of Judaism, at what makes it infinitely valuable, we have to invest a great deal of intellectual, emotional, spiritual, as well as physical effort, putting ideas into action, actualizing potentials, through *mitzvot*.

The essential ingredient that we were never offered a taste of in Judaism was its modesty. That is what has kept it from being totally depreciated by a mass consumption that was effortless. The status of the Jewish woman in a Torah lifestyle has been preserved on the high and powerful level that it was always on because of the modesty inherent in the role. Without it, there is a tremendous sinking, and the power, as we saw so starkly, becomes lost.

Remember that detestable little expression, "Women should be seen and not heard?" In Torah-true Judaism, we are striving for the reverse. The aim is not to wrap women up in rolls of adhesive tape so that no one will ever see them. The stress, however, is on developing inner beauty, and not focusing on externals. What is internal, what is hidden and lasting and what requires an enormous amount of effort to develop, is what is valued. So many of the superficial social games we used to play are absent. Voices are coming from deep within, and so that is where the attention gets focused.

The goal of Judaism is to have the voice that comes straight from the heart of a Jewish woman penetrate every imprisoned heart that still yearns to be set free. Jewish women were created along with Jewish men to be lights to the world; to make clear the way to come close to God and derive the greatest and deepest pleasures from life. Yet for some time now, many Jewish women have not even heard their own voices speaking. We've been listening to the loud and pervasive voices of those raised with values foreign to our own, which have affected us deeply.

I hope that somehow, you will hear my voice now, Barbara, as I finally found something I wanted to say. And I pray that one day, God willing, I will hear yours.

January 15, 1985

"Motherhood"

The most valuable work,

Gets the lowest pay.

In this topsy-turvy world,

Today.

Receiving next to nothing,

For all you do?

Someday all will wish,

They were as rich,

As you.

February 17, 1985

Dear Leah,

It's been a long time since I've gotten a letter back from you, but I still can't give up trying to reach you.

Leah, I have to share with you something I just learned yesterday. Like I've written to you, the guidelines in Judaism are based upon an understanding that the actions we do with our bodies have an effect upon our souls. So the food we eat and even *how* we eat it affects us spiritually.

The directions about which food is kosher to eat, I've learned, were not made up arbitrarily. When I started to study some of the principles behind the laws, tiny fragments of the extraordinarily intelligent design involved became apparent.

As just one example, all animals that are aggressors, like most jungle animals and birds of prey, are forbidden for consumption by Jews. Their predatory tendencies would somehow actually be harmful to us. And, as usual, scientific research, racing to catch up to the wisdom already available in the Torah, has "just discovered" that the raised level of hormones present in predatory animals can have a deleterious effect on human bodies. (The scientific research makes no comment about our souls.) Why pigs are not considered kosher is an even *more* enlightening subject, which I'll save for another time!

Well anyway, yesterday I learned another very interesting detail about how we determine what is kosher to eat. Even among peaceful birds, only the ones that are considered healthy enough to live one year are classified as fit for kosher consumption. But how do we determine if a given bird is healthy enough to live through the year?

The bird is put in a river flowing downstream. If we see that the bird is strong enough to swim against the current, it signifies that the bird has the strength to live out the year. If it is not strong enough to swim upstream against the downward current, we should save its life, but it is not a bird that we can ritually slaughter to eat. What does all that mean? Why am I telling you all this?

These guidelines, like every guideline in Judaism, unfold deep truths about life to us. Leah, we are those birds. We were both trying to swim upstream against a current that was relentlessly pushing us downward. For years, we frantically struggled not to drown in the scum that was overpowering us, but we were always on the verge. We both wanted to escape from a life that made little sense and had little beauty left in it.

Judaism is trying to teach us that the ones who are truly healthy are the ones who are strong enough to swim against the merciless current. We are the ones who *could* live.

Today, there is a lot of talk about a book that just came out, *The Closing of the American Mind* by Allan Bloom (Jewish, of course!). Have you read it? He writes how young people now have "powerful images of what a perfect body is and pursue it incessantly. But deprived of guidance, they no longer have any image of a perfect soul and hence do not long to have one."

His words really hit home, except for the last part, that they "do not long to have one." It may not be a *conscious* longing, but that longing is the first thing submerged in the struggle to overcome the powerful downward current. But it is a longing still felt, nevertheless. It is a longing expressed in all the symptoms of anxious tension, mental illness, escape into drugs, and yes, also in eating disorders.

We may have had no image of what a perfect soul was, but we were in a *constant* state of longing for one.

How I wish you would come here and see what our heritage has to offer. How about just doing it for the sake of our friendship, which has lasted all these years, if nothing else?

December 4, 1985

"A Hellenist Left Standing"

It was the twenty-fifth of December,

And when she closes her eyes she remembers,

Just how it was.

A Jewish girl from Queens,

Had fulfilled her secret dreams,

Decorating that bright, forbidden tree.

A Jewish girl from Queens,

Had fulfilled her secret dreams.

She helped hang tinsel merrily.

Her boyfriend's family,

Was friendly as could be.

They had fun watching her delight.

Her boyfriend's family,

Was friendly as could be.

By the fireplace they sang carols that night.

Then they piled into the car.

It wasn't very far.

Greetings called to those they'd pass.

Then they piled into the car.

It wasn't very far.

Each year the family went to Midnight Mass.

But there in a church pew,

She didn't know what to do,

As everyone else bent down to kneel.

But there in a church pew,

She didn't know what to do.

In those moments was her future sealed?

Alone, trembling, she stood,

Still uncertain if she should.

What stopped her from kneeling in that place?

Alone, trembling, she stood,

Still uncertain if she should.

The word "Jew" was stamped on her face.

The twenty-fifth makes her remember,

Because it's Kislev,* not December.

She almost fell, like Hellenists of old.

The twenty-fifth makes her remember,

Because it's Kislev, not December.

Once she, too, chose tinsel, not the gold.

So radiant, hidden away.

A golden light, still pure today.

Flashing bulbs have a different glow.

So radiant, hidden away.

A golden light, still pure today.

Her Jewish home shines with a warmth she didn't know.

For now ten years have passed.

Ten Chanukahs spin by so fast.

And as my children light, my past becomes less real.

For now ten years have passed.

Ten Chanukahs spin by so fast.

Standing by lights, I whisper thanks I didn't kneel.

(*Chanukah is on the 25th of the Jewish month of Kislev.)

Chapter Fifteen: 1986-1987

April 8, 1986

Aunt Trudy came to our Passover s*eder*. I still can't believe she was really here. She came bringing Uncle Irving, along with the same brand of smelly cigars he's been smoking for decades, and their sons, my cousins, Jack and Ted, who were not married to Jewish wives.

They were all taking a tour together—some kind of "package-deal" whizzing them through Italy, Greece, and Israel in record time. But Aunt Trudy planned the trip so she would wind up in Israel for the beginning of the holiday of Passover, and she was hoping to be by family for a s*eder*.

We were what she meant by family since we're the only members of our whole extended family that live in Israel. So even though they had all been forewarned, I'm sure, that I'm now a "religious fanatic," they very bravely came marching in.

At first, they all looked a bit taken aback by how small and simple this dwelling is. Well, it's not exactly up to American standards, but we have all we need, my husband assured them. By making do with less, as some saying goes, we get more of what really counts. But how do you get along without "home entertainment," my Cousin Ted asked me privately—no sound system, no home computer, no VCR—not even a *TV*? "What do you *do*?"

"Oh we've got plenty of home entertainment," I whispered back, with a smile.

I caught them watching with disbelief when my six-year-old daughter divided up the chocolate bar they gave her. She broke it into equal pieces for her siblings, saving the smallest piece for herself. And when my four-year-old son offered his uncle and cousins his own extra *yarmulkes* as *his* gift to them, they accepted their presents with great big grins. The *yarmulke* really did wonders for Uncle Irving's nearly bald head.

Little by little, the true value of our home began to unfold before their eyes. And when we all sat down together for the *seder* that evening, nobody was able to take their eyes off the four beautiful children seated eagerly around the table, with their bright, holiday clothes and radiant faces.

Look at these four creations I've helped to bring into this world! What a responsibility I've been entrusted with—these little bodies, housing tremendous souls. I have to always try to think clearly, choosing every moment a way that helps each one to grow. They are watching nearly everything I do, and they see what I don't do. Is there any profession that requires more thinking on the job than being a mother?

I've heard people say plenty of times that they don't want to impose values on their children. But isn't that in itself a value? Aren't they then deciding to leave their children prey to the values floating around school and the street? I think the real reason they don't want to transmit their values to their children is that they're not clear themselves about the values they hold. And children can sniff out exactly what's going on beneath the surface. They know whenever their parents are wishy-washy.

"Why is this night different from all other nights?" the children were singing, in turn. *Different from all other nights.* So different from all those other nights I had once longed for from my bedroom window. Yes, different, but revitalized. *This is* what I was really longing for. This real Judaism, this real life that had been drained away. A night as alive as this.

- 195 -

And why, I was wondering, is this Jewish people different from all other people? That's a question, my neighbor, Mrs. Goldberg, knows well. She is a woman not afraid to show the numbers on her arm, which show she's different. She told me that when she was finally liberated from Bergen-Belsen concentration camp, at age sixteen, she returned alone to the town in Hungary where she had lived before her parents and brothers and sisters had been taken away from her. She was the only one from her family who survived. As she approached the street where her home had been, non-Jewish neighbors, who she had thought were their friends years before, called out to her from their windows. "*What!* Some of you are *still* left?"

Yes, some of us are still left. And we are still carrying within us an eternal light, preserving a consciousness of God that is impossible to extinguish.

My husband's words called me back. He was reading from the Passover *Haggadah*, a few paragraphs before the meal. "In each and every generation, a person has to see himself as if he has left Egypt."

The *seder* is not meant as just a historical commemoration. The *seder* is designed to show us that going out of Egypt is a continuous process.

It is primarily directed to us where we are today, and it can enable us to see how we have left our own personal slavery—as if *I* have been freed from slavery. When I served the meal, reminders of my own personal slavery lay spread out across the s*eder* table. Once my arms, my legs, my entire brain was bound up in chains to food.

And the text continues, "Not only our ancestors did the Holy One redeem, *but us too…*"

Food is just not so important anymore. Now I fill up pretty

quickly. My life is brimming over with an adoring husband, four beautiful children, an inner calmness—a soul at peace. How much food do I need?

I think it was evident to everyone present at this *Seder* that what's great about Judaism is no longer only the gefilte fish, the chopped liver, or the chicken soup. At this *Seder* table, I think even Aunt Trudy saw that there were more important things to talk about than fluffy matzo balls.

I felt like sitting there around our table was my past, my present, and my future. At this celebration of the struggle for freedom, a timeless exodus was unfolding, a reality more amazing to me than magical fairy tales ever were.

This is Wonderland. My life has become a song of joy. It is my turn to read out loud from the *Haggadah*, and it is hard to believe these words were always there at each Passover *Seder*, but I had never really seen them until this time. "...From the trash heaps, He lifts the needy—to seat them with nobles, with the nobles of his people. He transforms the barren woman into a happy mother of children..."

Just as the Jews discovered when they began their exodus, emancipation from bondage is only the beginning of a long redemptive process. Our bodies are vessels. And our bodies can turn from defiled vessels into vessels that can actually hold pure things. I was a defiled and a broken vessel. There are still some scars left, proving it, but they are healing. Thank God, they are fading away.

Before leaving Egypt, the Jews were directed to go into their houses and eat one last meal together with all their family members. So the first law the Jewish people as a whole were ever given, was to get together with family for a gathering like our *Seder*. The family is our basic building block. It was the first step we took thousands of years ago to solidify our nation, and it is the first step we are taking again now to rebuild our nation—from millions of ashes.

After Uncle Irving, my two cousins and their wives had already gotten into their rented car for the return trip to their hotel in Jerusalem, Aunt Trudy turned to thank me one last time. "In such a small house, I've never seen a bunch of little children behave so well," she began. "You have something here I just don't see any more nowadays. Something I'd almost forgotten." And then her throaty voice cracked, "Joanne," she said, with eyes streaming, "This is the richest and happiest family I've ever seen."

It is easy to sail away with a thousand more thoughts about this Passover experience, but enough is enough for now. Life is far too short. When will I ever have them all small again like this? Their little mouths are open. They are hungry for me to give them what will last.

July 21, 1986

"What a Dream I Had, Leah"

Here you are standing here beside me, with a look of scorn.

How have these past years made all your plans go wrong?

Once we were two girls laughing, we were full of schemes,

　　Now your eyes just reflect shattered dreams.

Before you were born,

　　The angels taught you all you had to know.

Before you were here,

The angels told you how life would appear.

Before you came,

The angels sang you songs that filled your soul.

Before you were born,

The puzzle pieces of this world looked whole.

Why do I try to give excuses for the woman's role?

You've got the answers buried in your soul.

You watch me with my children—living proof the years
have passed.

So many men have gone through your life—nothing lasts.

Before you were born,

The angels taught you all you had to know.

Before you were here,

The angels told you how life would appear.

Before you came,

The angels sang you songs that filled your soul.

Before you were born,

The puzzle pieces of this world looked whole.

And now you're standing here beside me, wondering what
to do.

I have lit the Shabbos candles, now it's up to you.

Your hands cover both eyes, in hopes they'll hide the tears.

Inside something's released, you haven't felt in years.

Before you were born,

The angels sang you songs that filled your soul.

Before you were born,

The puzzle pieces of this world looked whole.

Your eyes light up.

Was it the Shabbos candles that you saw?

Or did you hear the song?

The one they sang you years before.

It was March 7, 1987. Over forty young women packed into a small, dimly-lit room. Everyone was sitting cross-legged on the floor. Our first "Women's Forum" meeting was taking place, and I couldn't believe so many women had shown up. All I did was put up a few posters. The views expressed by feminists years back have seeped down deep into our minds. Now we are questioning what we accepted.

"First, I want to thank everyone for coming," I began. "It is very important that women get together to share ideas and goals and problems. I want to begin by reading you a story someone once wrote. It is called: 'A Dollhouse Reality.'

"When a little girl receives her first miniature kit of make-up, her first Little Miss Happy Homemaker ironing board set, or her first Betsy-Wetsy doll, she does not realize the huge price that she will eventually have to pay for them…But it's too late. Squirrels aren't running by, treasure-hunting has lost its original appeal, and by now her own little Betsy-Wetsy has grown up. She's reading magazines that have catchy little phrases like, 'A Diamond is Forever', smeared all over them.

"Maybe it is hard for you to believe that I'm the one who wrote that story, back when I was seventeen years old. But it's really not so hard for me to believe it, because I still think that what I wrote then is true. Occupation housewife is an empty and meaningless role. It is no wonder that we rebelled in the 60's and 70's. We were terrified of a future where shiny floors and a perfect three-layer cake were the ultimate goals.

"But, we thought the solution to the emptiness would be getting a career. That would make our lives fulfilled. Yet as more and more women are finding out today, careers have also not filled up the emptiness. So what *is* the answer?

"Well, in typical Jewish style, maybe we will be able to answer that question through asking more questions. Why *did* so many women watch their dollhouse dreams turn into nightmares? What legitimate suppressed needs sparked the feminist revolution? And why do so many women today— even religious women—feel trapped and miserable?

"The answer to all these questions can be found in the answer to a question which people often like to ask me (either directly or indirectly): Can a woman who loves to think become a homemaker? The answer is: *In order* to become a successful Jewish homemaker, I learn again and again to my amazement, a woman *has* to love to think.

"She needs to be constantly alert to see how every small sub-goal she is involved with during the day is tied *directly* to her ultimate goal. She has to be at work every minute, tying threads throughout all her actions. Without constantly re-connecting to the reality that there is a God who gave us directions for living life fully, occupation Jewish homemaker gets washed down to occupation housewife. A life with almost all the light drained out of it.

"We have to train our minds to remember our highest goals constantly, because otherwise, every minute we are forgetting them. It is not like you see life's purpose and the struggle is over.

"Now I know what to do, but that doesn't mean I am always doing it. It's like waiting in a long line at a bank, reading a book. When I finally get up to the teller's window and he asks what I would like, imagine if I tell him not to bother me because I'm busy reading an interesting chapter. We get so absorbed by distractions along the way that we think that's all there is. We forget why we are here to begin with.

"The struggle is to keep our actions, our bodies, in tune with our souls, sensitive to its calls. The struggle is to keep waking up to a greater and greater level of awareness all the time, of what we are doing it all for. What that usually comes down to in real-life terms, is a struggle to stifle that highly contagious yawn.

"Two months ago, we actually built a dollhouse for our children. I watch them sometimes as they play with it, moving around all the little people and furniture. Their eyes look dreamy. May their sweet dreams never sour, like mine once did. May they never become terrified of what their future will be, like I once was. I know they can see how happy I am. But they can't *possibly* imagine the intensity of this fulfillment.

"Whether we are having sweet dreams or nightmares, we are still asleep. We feel like dozing off…it is soooo comfortable. Waking up takes effort.

"And yet, when we do manage to open up our eyes, we see that what we are doing here is nothing smaller than extracting the hidden essence of everything and every person we're with (including ourselves). Then a whining child with a runny nose and a smelly diaper invariably interrupts our lofty thoughts by spilling a bowl of spaghetti with ketchup plop-on-top of the words we are writing.

"Though they may seem trivial to an outsider, we are taking difficult tests every second. We have to use our minds, and also our hearts, at optimum capacity, just to recognize the tests.

"It is not such a struggle to purify oneself and feel uplifted in a monastery. But in a messy, noisy *kitchen*, now *that* is something.

"The Divine Presence, we learn from the Torah, is in a feminine form. We have to stay awake to see Her fill our homes, or else we'll miss Her. She is The Dollhouse Reality. But I did not see that years ago. That's what was missing. Revealing Her Presence makes all the difference in the world."

September 11, 1986

Dear Mom,

Shalom! How are you?

I hope you're feeling well.

Thank God, everyone is fine.

And I have some news to tell.

It's hard for me to write you,

These words which should cause joy.

Soon we will have, God willing,

A brand new girl or boy.

Already I can picture,

The look that's on your face.

Daughter dear, must you produce,

The whole human race?

I'm thinking of your health, you'd say,

With genuine concern.

You want to save the Jewish People,

But give someone else a turn.

Your body needs a rest, my dear,

Why can't you take a break?

If you will not listen to me,

Do it for the children's sake.

Of course I love each little face.

I treasure every one.

But don't forget, you're still *my* child,

And I'm worried about you, hon.

Physically, emotionally,

And financially too,

Children are very draining.

What will be left of you?

And then come your closing words.

Mom, they always pierce through me.

Just remember: What's important,

Is quality, not quantity.

The other arguments never swayed me,

But this one would sting.

Quality, not quantity.

That *does* have a good ring.

Your words never leave me, Mom.

They won't go away.

But this time as I write to you,

I now know what to say.

Better quality than quantity,

But which one must I lose?

Who says that you can't have both?

Who says I have to choose?

I don't see why I should settle,

And sell myself so short.

I'm trying to *make* good human beings.

This isn't merchandise I've bought.

This job would be too much for me,

If it all fell on my shoulders.

Dan and I, we do our parts,

Yet it is God who grows them older.

You're worried if we'll have enough,

But can't you see my wealth?

I am *glowing* from my diamonds,

And these children *give* me health.

Do you think more pleasure will drain me?

Then let me say one thing -

All that I can give to them,

Does not compare with what they bring.

Why don't you understand me?

Really *you're* the one to blame.

You filled my life with so much love, Mom,

I want to do the same.

I'll keep wishing you will share my joy.

I hope someday you'll see,

All my children are an expression,

Of all the love you put in me.

September 14, 1987

I went back for a visit to the States this past summer. My parents have gotten older, too, of course. My mother is not so well now, and they can't come anymore to see all their grandchildren in Israel. So we brought the children to them.

My parents are packing up now to leave New York and move to a retirement community in Florida. They had kept my room just as it was when I left, years before. My Dad asked me to go through all my papers, which were stuffed in the big, brown, wooden bureau, and to dump whatever I didn't want into the garbage.

So I sat down, and for hours I read through a lot of old papers describing a me that used to be. Report cards, commendations, awards, and recommendation letters, all finally on their way out. The wonder girl was buried in a bunch of old liquor boxes by the trash bin.

In high school, I was the one voted most likely to succeed. Who could have known then what real success meant?

I got rid of five full cartons! About half a boxful of letters, diaries, and journals came back to Israel with me. I know it's not a major archaeological finding, but here it is.

After reading through all those papers in my parents' home, I couldn't resist making some phone-calls that night. I wanted to try and track down some of the people who had gone through my life, and find out what happened to them.

Stan Cohen, from high school, my only *Jewish* boyfriend (the one who had been into Christian Science), had married a minister's daughter. Bill McDonald, my Baptist boyfriend in med school, became an accomplished psychiatrist.

Following my phone-call to Michael, he and his wife, Rachel, came over to visit with me and my husband and our children. Michael is now a business consultant. His wife is Jewish, a Harvard graduate, a doctor. And we looked so incredibly similar, she might have been me.

There was also someone else that might have been me. My closest friend, Leah, who I wasn't able to reach. She died in a mental hospital this past June from anorexia nervosa.

December 10, 1987

"The Sculptress"

Shut up. Shut up already. Let me

think about something else please,

besides how much I should eat at

my next meal and the one after

that and for breakfast tomorrow

morning. It's enough already. Let

me stop thinking about it. Let me

think about something else please.

There is still a sculptress

but

no longer the clink-clank of my robot arm

stretching my robot hand out to touch

a machine

to get a sandwich out

and in.

I thought skinny meant freedom, not

when five bagels later

the sirens of terror would go off

caught, caught. And they'd get more and more

hateful

and I could not get them to stop.

All she wanted was for her body to be free to run down a
hill again.

She wanted to be free like a dancer

and yet by the end, she was unable

to take a step

without it being pre-set, pre-planned

in that repetitive program

that was being run over and over

in her head.

She could not trust anyone or anything

not even the words

on this page -

(if she had been reading them then)

because she knew

that they

were all set out to make her

FAT.

The world was grossly stuffed with big, fat lies.

And she wanted to be the mommy in her life. Sick from
being so

good, yet she did not

want to

be a

bad girl.

She reasoned, it is too scary to become a woman now, if I

eat one piece more of that heavy, heavy food my hips

will begin to ooze out over the sides of the chair.

I don't like twisting my head back to look

at that girl-woman anorexic. Confused

about what was important in life, too many

signals to read, too many demands she

could see through—but not that clearly. She was looking
for

me now

and meanwhile, she was carving out a message

with her body,

so that when somebody would find it, it would look

like her starving soul.

Chapter Sixteen: 1988

January 2, 1988

Dear Twilly,

I came into the kitchen and flicked on the light because I need to write to you again. It is three o'clock in the morning, but there is one last entry I have to make on the pages in the back of my journal, still left open. And now I just looked up at the date I wrote on the top of this page. It is over twenty years from the day that I first started writing to you.

Chana, my littlest, woke me up to nurse her, as usual, in the middle of the night. I somehow often do my clearest thinking at these private meetings we have. A half-hour ago, while nursing Chana back to sleep, and with all the other people in our house sound asleep, I got a glimpse of a single thread that I had never seen before. It's a thread that seems to tie my whole life together.

This afternoon my friend, Miriam, had come over to use my washing machine. Her washer broke down yesterday, so she is really "up a creek" as she puts it. While she was loading her laundry into the machine, I started telling her that in trying to put together all these pages about my life, I was becoming confused by the abrupt changes I had made. There were two important questions that I had, but I could only ask Miriam one of them.

I told Miriam, who had become a convert to Judaism when she was twenty-one, how I had been re-reading some of the feminist literature that I had read years ago. The book, *My Mother, Myself,* left a big impression that was bothering me. It said that a woman needs to become independent from her mother before marrying, or else "she will never be her own person." A woman needs to live by herself for a while, and become both physically and emotionally separated from her mother.

"Women in the society from which we came accept this implicitly nowadays," I said. "Dan and I share a wonderful marriage, thank God, but still…maybe what they are saying is true… maybe I should have become more independent before I got married, maybe I did get married out of weakness."

"Of course you did," Miriam smiled at me. "That's why people get married. The Torah explains that people seek what they have lost. Our search for a soul-mate runs parallel to our search for the spiritual. An unmarried person cannot be spiritually complete. And how does the author *know* women are meant to live on their own for an interim period? Why *do* we have to have that 'single scene' stage? People need familial support.

"But on the other hand, Bracha, we really can't help *but* be independent. God relates to you as an individual, not as only part of a married couple. Each woman has her own absolutely unique relationship with God. Each woman has her own individually designed tests in life. There's no getting around it. That doesn't mean, though, that a woman needs to live mentally or physically apart from her family. 'Living on your own' teaches you to be selfish. And we all fell for that. We accepted 'being selfish' as a kind of noble and necessary trait to acquire.

"The Torah way is for both women and men to live with their families until they get married and begin a new family. And then they will have not just a nice, neat nuclear family, hopefully, but a big and boisterous extended one.

"And God knows exactly how people operate, Bracha! At the age of twelve, a girl becomes Bat Mitzvah. At thirteen, a boy becomes Bar Mitzvah. *At that critical point*, girls change into women and boys change into men, in Jewish terms. They begin to take responsibility for their lives. The teenagers growing up in our community go through inner turmoil and awakening, but they are still always on the path of learning about the wisdom of life. So they never feel suddenly stranded and lost. They never go through all that *unnecessary pain* I went through as an adolescent in the years before I learned about Judaism. Didn't you experience anything like that too, Bracha?"

Miriam's words this afternoon had only the whirring of the washing machine for a "background soundtrack," but they still must have gotten through to me. They were probably still moving around in my head making further nerve fiber connections, when Chana woke me up.

I woke up, clearly facing the female skeleton in my closet. My most disturbing question, the one I had still not asked. *How had I changed from an anorexic into an observant Jew practically overnight? Was* it just an "easy out" for me, like my brother-in-law is still insisting to this day? His view made so much sense. I never did give him a good rebuttal to his claims. I never had one. Was it as it appeared, another way for me to avoid making decisions, letting a "system of laws" make the decisions for me? Was it a way to continue to avoid growing up?

I sat there, holding Chana in the darkness of my bedroom, and I began singing softly, "Young girls are April, with rainbows and changes. One day they grow up, and April is over forever." And my eyes filled up. Anorexia. Try to stay in control. Run again. Run my life. That was all *unnecessary pain*. Growing up doesn't *have* to be like that. The real world doesn't have to be scary.

My Tree—I was so terrified of it dying. My Tree of Life, so beautiful and strong. My Tree was cut down, but still there were all those scattered leaves to find. Like the Hasidic tales I would cling to. Dragging them along, wherever I went.

I feel like Dorothy waking up at the end of *The Wizard of Oz*, recognizing all the familiar characters that appeared before. Only for me, it's the nightmare I had earlier that appeared in drab gray, and this real world I've woken up to is in living color.

Collecting leaves, then finding the roots, then planting seeds. I am understanding. Now I know why I wanted to put all this writing together. Now that the pieces are here before me, threaded together, I can see that there is a thread. I am beginning to understand my life.

Dancing, skipping, skinny Joanne became twelve, and began expanding uncontrollably. Physically and spiritually, there were suddenly no more clear-cut lines. And there was nothing to do about it. It was uncontrollable.

Growing up meant boys started following you home from school to find out things meant to be kept private. Growing up meant being tough. Growing up meant learning to play new games I didn't like. Learning how to be phony. You just had to.

At the very same time that my body became uncontrollable, so did life. It stopped making sense. Before then, my questions had answers. And then suddenly all the absolutes vanished. God had to be given up along with all my dolls. But I did not know what to do with the soul I still felt I had.

Overnight, had my soul become useless and been replaced? Now there was only this new meaningless, valueless life I was being handed. No choice but to become a soul-less adult. I tried to become one…but that persistent soul kept re-emerging, desperately searching for what could sustain it.

Desperately searching. What does that remind me of? *All those eating binges! Desperately searching* for more and more. Never feeling satisfied—never getting filled up—it felt bottomless. The hunger wouldn't go away. *How could it?* Not my body's hunger *or* my soul's hunger! Oh—I don't believe this—that's *exactly* what we find in the Torah—everything that exists on a physical level is occurring on a spiritual level *at the very same time!*

And I just realized that the physical and spiritual are not merely *metaphorically* similar—like I was thinking when I wrote the poem about anorexia—they are *precise reflections*! *Not only* do the actions I do with my body affect my soul, *also what I do with my soul affects my body.* I became anorexic *because* my soul was starving.

Now I understand why I wasn't really getting "in control" of my body again with all that rigid dieting. I was only training myself not to listen to my healthy appetite. Just like I was trying not to listen to my healthy soul.

I did not eat in response to physical hunger signals, like I am able to do now. I almost never felt those signals. I suppressed my hunger, just like I had to suppress the hunger in my soul that was too painful to feel.

But then, those frantic binges came. My needs pouring out with no stop. Even stealing. Look at that! I was so obviously craving real parameters. And isn't that exactly *why* the physical and spiritual are parallel? What my body was doing was *meant as a message to me*, about what was going on in my soul. Spiritual struggles *are* expressed through physical means! How else?

Hey, did the Japanese therapist see this way back then? Is that why he thought spiritual sustenance would solve my overt eating disorder problem too? I think, in a way, I must have understood it, too, at some point because I was even able to write poems about it, but not on as conscious a level as when I woke up now.

Food, our most intimate physical craving—that actually becomes a part of our very beings—seems destined to be laden with a lot of emotional messages. For one thing, food tastes good, even when the rest of life doesn't. I could get away from my expanding misery by losing myself in those basic gratifying sensations for a little while. I could still count on the food to be pleasurable. And, I really had nothing else as pleasurable that I could look forward to after eating.

On the other side of the coin, by dieting like crazy, I could at least work on "perfecting" my body, avoiding the real transcendence that I didn't know how to pursue. Also, by suppressing my hunger, my body could actually become like a girl's again. Of course I was afraid to grow up. I did not see any place in the world for my soul to grow up.

The Torah's guidelines did not offer me an escape from my problems. They provided the direct solution. I guess I sensed this, but I never saw this clearly how they were connected before.

It must have clicked now because of my conversation with Miriam earlier. Growing up does not *have* to mean allowing your soul to be replaced—by nothing. I didn't feel free back then. I was paralyzed with terror in a world without direction. In that pervasive darkness, I had no idea why I kept bumping into walls and getting hurt. Now that I know where to turn, I really *can* be much more in control. I like taking responsibility for my life. Who knew it was supposed to be a pleasure?

Judaism freed me to grow up. But how? "Judaism explains

how to be good in a more detailed way than any other religion," a mentor said to me once. More details. *So what?* I still don't understand why those plain words felt like the long-lost key to my locked-up soul. I don't even *like* details. I like making connections between things. Details make distinctions; they separate. Who wants to get bogged down by details? Silly details. Oh, that's it. These were not silly details.

These details would not be meaningless. Because the picture they were all coming together to form wasn't meaningless. And not only that, but from the details I could actually extract the essence. That's the only way I could get *at* the essence. So there's the kernel of truth from the feminist book I had been re-reading about the importance of making separations. Making clear distinctions *enabled* me to make genuine connections.

And also, the details are the practical steps I have to make in order to genuinely get off the ground.

These details were what I was craving because I always wanted to fly. I wanted to soar off into the heavens like Peter Pan, like Mary Poppins. But I was also afraid of flying. That's because it's scary to fly without guidelines. I wanted to fly, but like all the other confused ones around, I was terrified with no way to get back down to earth safely.

I vaguely knew that somehow the spiritual and physical realms were tied together. I knew I needed some kind of connection to the ground. And strong spiritual muscles would help for graceful landings. Yes, that's what I always wanted: inner muscles so well developed that my movements could flow. Not jerky gestures responding to warped commands. To be able to run, to fly, to be able to dance. I wanted the freedom of a mind and an opened heart, in control of its body. Could that be the ultimate dance there is?

Oh Mary Poppins, I actually believed I would be able to just soar right up there alongside you. But it turned out, all you really did was help me to crash. Couldn't you have shown me and all the millions of other children who put their trust in you how wonderful *real* life was? Why fill us up with fantasies?

Oh, I know why. Because true life wasn't good enough. Real life was the letdown experienced coming out of the movie theater. What a pathetic, jarring contrast. Life was unbearably empty after fanciful productions. So in order not to face how boring regular life was, we had to keep running back to get lost in more fantasies. I get it now. All the unreal fantasies are the opiate of the masses!

Overeating is a part of that habituating fantasy-linked behavior. Fancifully wishing that my actions won't produce any negative consequences. I think nearly everyone develops some kind of addiction. Desperate to escape, and then even more disappointed afterward. The addictions feed on themselves.

But it doesn't have to be that way. Fake heroes like Mary Poppins taught us that the best parts of life are not real. But the best parts of life were just never presented. The spiritual pleasures had been discarded. Practically the only thrills offered us were from artificial flavorings and additives…from poisonous fluff. Food, Judaism, Life—all sneakily devitalized. I guess plants might be able to still keep growing if Diet Colas were poured on them, but they certainly wouldn't blossom the way they would if they were watered instead with simple unpolluted water.

It appears as if all the fluffy stuff, the illusory distractions, like fame and fortune and prestige, are important. But before you know it, we'll have to throw all that make-believe stuff back into the box anyway. Even Boardwalk and Park Place, too. Soon they'll all "magically" disappear.

We just can't accept, though, that nothing will remain from entire lifetimes. There *has* to be something permanent in this throwaway society. We *know* it. Within each of us there is a still small voice that won't give up insisting something lasts.

The voice comes from within all the empty vessels.

What finally fills my vessel, nurtures what always lined its inner walls. Each morsel of true nourishment enlivens something that was already present, but dormant. It sensitizes the essence which was once implanted there. My true essence was hidden under layers of dirt. I am still peeling off these layers, and as I do, with a wonder distilled from childhood, I can recognize my true self.

I am a woman who loves to run. I dance. I hang laundries. I wash off bruises. I tell bedtime stories. I live in a desert, which doesn't look like one anymore.

The restrictive binding of my outer shroud has mostly unraveled. I've been working on a new tapestry. It has golden fibers entwined with ordinary fabric, an outer self and inner essence being woven together. The days have a rich texture that is *not* elusive. And there are moments when I can fly, like this one. With wings caressing a singular thread.

This may be a world of illusions, but it is transformed every time I bite in, and really taste. What seems foolish, like becoming a giver, degrading, like becoming a homemaker, or even foolish, like becoming closer to God, really turns out the opposite. It *all* turns out the opposite.

We are here to experience life's deepest pleasures, but we

imagine we're just meant to be comfortable. We think it's a man's world, but we learn from Judaism that the essence of this world is feminine. We imagine that Jews have a history cloaked in darkness, but we are drenched in light. The Jewish guidelines keep us somewhat separated from other people, and yet paradoxically, our role is to be unifiers. We imagine our physical appearances are of utmost importance, but things are *not* how they appear. And it is so wondrous that through the decay within a person's life, like in the decomposition of each seed in the ground, a new life can emerge.

Every person feels separate from every other person, but really we *are* connected. We imagine we are just bodies, but *really we are souls*.

It's an inside-out world. But now I see that the purpose of life is to pierce through the veils. Peel off the outer shells. There is a very bitter rind sometimes. It is always a struggle to reveal the ultimate, lasting sweetness concealed underneath.

The purpose of life is to see through the facade of physicality to all the spiritual layers present. Behind the mirage, there really *is* a Golden Mountain, infinitely greater than the "mountain top" of disillusionment at the Harvard Garden Party I once got to attend.

There *is* a pure awareness in the heart, but it can become obscured, it can get desensitized.

The purpose of my life is to keep waking up like this.

What was I dreaming about before I heard Chana's cries early this morning? It's a new dream that keeps coming back. About thousands of pairs of *tefillin* (phylacteries men wear on their heads during a Jewish prayer service) that will be found someday. They are lying in the bottom of the Hudson River. They are *tefillin* that were thrown overboard from ships jammed with Jews. The ships were headed toward America at the turn of the 20th Century, when my grandparents came.

The Jewish people were carrying with them an extremely heavy tradition that they, generally, did not understand. They honestly did not know why they should continue holding onto it. Why did so many Jews toss their legacy overboard, before even going ashore? They were ignorant of Jewish wisdom, and they were convinced that their heritage would weigh them down in a land of *freedom*.

But again and again, the Jewish *neshama* will try to get up. It will search for excitement, for love, for wisdom, for nourishment. Not knowing where to look, but searching anyway. For all the lost pieces that were thrown away. Thrown away…

Like the half-eaten sandwiches! Could that have been what I was trying to do in a crazy kind of way? Hunting through the garbage, through the sewage. Looking for something still left over.

Both my body and my soul had healthy demands. They were both craving healthful sustenance; the pure gifts God provides. But they were subsisting mostly on poisons. We need both spiritual as well as physical nourishment that comes directly from its Source, before it's been depleted of its vitality.

And within us *always remains* the potential to become re-sensitized. And also *never completely lost* are the valuable instructions that detail how to respect and care for our souls, others' souls, and the bodies that house them.

All at once my seemingly senseless behavior is making sense to me. I was acting out the inner craving that I had been expressing in just less bizarre forms for years. And no amount of intellectual or psychological analysis of the problem could help solve it. *I was searching for something that might still have value.* Something that could still be redeemed. Even if that meant stealing it from others, and even if that meant recovering it from drenched refuse. There was something that had been thrown away that I knew I needed desperately in order to live. It was a message from my *neshama* to my body, crying out, best it could. And it was purposely being made more and more sickeningly clear.

We never really know what's going on inside another person. Nobody would ever guess all this was going on inside of me. Every human being is filled with many contradictory motivations, most of them hidden, even to the individual involved. We *can* know though, that within each and every person, no matter how covered up, there is a God-given hole. And an unrelenting need to have it filled.

January 3, 1988

In re-reading the book, *A Tzaddik in Our Time*, I just noticed something that Rabbi Aryeh Levin had written:

"A holy duty lies on every one of us to record for himself the details of all the events, incidents, and adventures in his life. In the Torah we read, 'from my own flesh I can perceive God' (Job 19:26). With a clear vision you can see His sure hand in the happenings of your own life."

January 8, 1988

"To the Rabbi's Wife"

Just what did you do?

I bet you never knew.

How did you do more

Than anyone before?

Well, we walked for hours on that cloudy day.

You let me spill out thoughts—I could never say.

Winding on and on, through all the narrow streets.

Jerusalem's hills carried our feet.

A cynic scared to feel

Can't believe God is real.

I'm fine. I'm A.O.K.

Then nervous laughter gave me away.

I'd seen enough psychologists, but oh, they never heard.

And with all my T.M. chanting, I said just one word.

But you *were* listening to me, so I began to talk.

I first used my real voice on that long, long walk.

Just what did you do?

It wasn't what you said.

You did not tell me.

You let me tell myself instead.

Brought up to the surface, my doubts didn't seem so black.

After I had let them out, I didn't ever want them back.

You saw me start to trust. You saw me lift a veil.

A real frozen heart melts much more than

in fairytales.

I never thanked you all these years,

But now I've got the chance.

You took the time to let me think,

And that's made all the difference.

You really listened. That's what's hard.

You didn't let me just go by.

You held the sky. I spread my wings.

Cocoon to butterfly.

About the Author

Bracha Goetz is the Harvard-educated author of over forty children's books, which portray life's deepest concepts in a delightfully simple way. She gives presentations based on her books for both children and adults, inspiring each uniquely beautiful soul to shine. Mrs. Goetz also works as a consultant, helping individuals, organizations, and businesses.

Please share your feedback about this memoir (or any of Bracha Goetz's picture books) at the website lovingly created by her children: www.goetzbookshop.com or email us at info@goetzbookshop.com. We love to hear from you!

You can download a free copy of The Pleasure Ladder chart from the website too. The Pleasure Ladder, created by Rabbi Noach Weinberg, provides a clear and empowering view of how to fill life with an abundance of pleasure.

Scan for
Pleasure Ladder

Made in the USA
Columbia, SC
25 June 2024

37544877R00126